bowl&fork

recipes you will love to eat

Anna Lisle

To Hughie

CONTENTS

FOREWORD

When Anna asked me to write the foreword for her new book, I must admit I was quite chuffed and honored to do this for her. I've known Anna for many years and what I most adore about her is that she is so down to earth and I think this really shines through in this cookbook. You can see that her food philosophy and inspiration has come from years of growing up on a farm. From one cook to another, I just love Anna's approach to food and cooking. This book isn't one to follow food trends; just wholesome, real food for real people—it's a cookbook that people will keep going back to.

Bowl&Fork is packed full of approachable, healthy, every day recipes. For me this book highlights true comfort food with her own twist. Best of all, it is real food that will satisfy and nourish you. There's a variety of recipes; some simple weeknight meals and some requiring a bit of time to prepare. There's a vast amount of multicultural influences—almost every recipe is inspired by something Anna has eaten or discovered on her travels such as the Mexican tortilla bowl, the Japanese-style salmon donburi, Chinese XO prawns and cider and cardamom poached pears.

These are recipes that people will adore; from a comforting and spicy bowl of prawn laksa to a baked side of salmon with yoghurt and herb crust. From braised beef cheeks in aromatic spices to a beautiful selection of vegetarian dishes such as caramelised miso tofu and, one of my favorites, roasted beetroot risotto. The salads in this book will surprise and delight even the biggest of carnivores, from parmesan kale to crunchy cauliflower, quinoa and almond salad. Anna hasn't forgotten those with a sweet tooth too. The balsamic figs, raspberry and apple crumble bake and rhubarb and pistachio fool will delight and excite tastebuds.

I think Anna will have a very long and fruitful future with her cooking. She is always so happy to be in the kitchen working away on new recipes. She is so passionate in her approach and the way she talks about food; it is a big part of her life and brings her so much joy. You can see that Anna loves how cooking and food connects people. It is so much more than just sustenance; especially in today's world, it's how families and friends come together.

This cookbook is a must for any passionate home cook who loves food as much as Anna. The recipes are easy to follow and the book is stylish with beautiful photography. I can guarantee that this book won't just be a coffee table book but a cookbook that will be well used with well-stained pages!

Luke Mangan
Celebrity Chef and Restaurateur

INTRODUCTION

Most people eat to live. I live to eat. Food is more than fuel for our bodies. It's how we connect with other cultures, it's the fabric that ties our family and friends together and it's also one of life's greatest comforts.

I find the process of cooking quite magical. You can take something so simple, like a sweet potato, toss it with olive oil and spices and after roasting, suddenly you create crunchy mouthfuls of happiness. I still remember the first time I made ricotta—things didn't start off well. I boiled the milk (rather than gently simmering) and then I ran out of vinegar but I kept going regardless, hopeful that it might just work. As I added a little vinegar, like magic, those gorgeous creamy clumps appeared. 10 minutes later, I was sitting on the bench, eating the warm ricotta straight out of the cloth. Slowly and deliberately, I ate the entire batch in complete awe. I couldn't even wait for it to drain.

My food philosophy is simple. I believe in eating whole foods—ingredients in their most nutritious and natural form; vegetables, fruits, whole grains, lean meats, seafood, legumes, nuts and seeds. I'm not interested in complicated cooking. I like simple dishes that can be eaten while perched at the kitchen bench with kids running around your feet or sitting on the couch, flicking through a magazine. This is where the idea for *Bowl & Fork* came from. It's the type of food you want to eat after a hard day in the office or when you've been running around after your kids. It's not hard to cook or plate up. Like many women (and men), I'm acutely aware of the pressures of body image. Add to that a family history of depression and I've always been conscious of the role food plays on one's mental and physical state. Listening to our bodies' needs makes more sense than setting up rules for what we can or cannot eat.

I'm happiest when armed with a basket and a pair of scissors, exploring the garden for herbs and vegetables to create a dish. As I look over the veggie patch, the possibilities are endless: beetroots, roasted, then pureed for a risotto, the leaves sautéed in butter and sprinkled with salt; perhaps fresh green beans, stir fried until crisp and tossed with honey and miso. I have a similar experience at the local gourmet grocer, sans the scissors and fresh air. Wherever I am, dreaming up a meal is my favorite time of the day. Well, that and coffee time.

I was 23 when I first realized the importance of cooking and food in my life. My brother, Hugh, passed away and during the months after he died, cooking was one of the few activities that gave me any joy or pleasure. To be in the kitchen, just chopping onions or stirring a pot of soup, was the only place that I felt at peace. It was during this time that I knew I had to change the direction of my life. With a background in journalism, I decided to merge my profession with my passion to become a restaurant critic with an online restaurant guide. Then came a stint on Channel 7's reality series *My Kitchen Rules*, together with my beautiful Mum, Cathy. From that experience, we finally had the confidence to launch our cooking school, *The Walcha Kitchen* and produce a handmade muesli and granola range. To be able to share my recipes through *Bowl & Fork* is an honor and a dream come true. For me, to cook and feed my family and friends fills me with an absolute, bursting happiness that nothing else equates to.

Bowl & Fork is a compilation of wholesome dishes that combine textures and flavors. This book is also an expression of my love for multicultural cooking—from a Mexican tortilla bowl and Japanese-style salmon donburi to a Middle Eastern freekeh and eggplant salad, rustic apple and raspberry crumble and a Thai black sticky rice pudding. These recipes will show you that there are no limits to the humble bowl. I also cook and eat according to the seasons. It's cheaper, tastier and I also love the notion of waiting until the best mangoes are available in summer rather than eating imported mangoes all year round. The recipes in this book are not designed to be followed like a bible; they're edible inspiration for creating dishes that work for you, that allow you to invest as much or as little time and energy as you'd like.

There are two types of cooks; those who follow recipes and those who don't. I fall into the latter which, when writing a cookbook, certainly creates certain challenges. I find following recipes restrictive. I often change halfway through a recipe, to throw in a bit of this, take out a bit of that. However, I know many great cooks who like to use instructions throughout the entire dish. In *Bowl & Fork*, I hope I appease both types of cooks.

As I look through my favorite recipes, I can't help noticing that I use certain ingredients over and over again. Like any other craftsman, you need the right tools to get started. As far as cornerstone staples go, I would recommend buying the best quality extra virgin olive oil you can afford. A good quality olive oil can make or break a dish. Tamari appears in many of my dishes. Unlike soy sauce, which is used widely in Asian cooking, tamari is a Japanese soy sauce that is made with no (or very little) wheat. I find tamari offers a more balanced flavor and is less salty. Tamari can be found in supermarkets, quite commonly in the health food aisle. When seasoning, I use sea salt as it has a finer, cleaner taste than most other salts and many of my recipes call for freshly ground pepper. While salt brings out and enhances the natural flavors in food, black pepper is really a spice that adds an additional layer of complexity. I love black pepper—I think it helps any dish. However, if you're impartial to it, just leave it out. Ground black pepper isn't really worth buying because once the hard, black shell of a peppercorn is cracked open, the aromas fade almost immediately.

A well-stocked pantry is essential, especially for the cook who comes home from work, without having had time to go to the supermarket. I try to buy the majority of my non-perishable ingredients in bulk, mostly because it's cheaper but also because I hate running out of an ingredient halfway through a recipe. My kitchen is influenced by ingredients from around the world so you may need a trip to your local Asian supermarket or gourmet grocer. White (shiro) miso, wasabi, Sichuan peppercorns, Sriracha (Thai hot chili sauce), mirin, Shaoxing wine, tahini (sesame seed paste), pomegranate molasses and sumac are a few ingredients I use often. They are excellent additions to any pantry.

I am enchanted by a perfectly outfitted kitchen with all the trimmings as much as the next person. The reality is, my kitchen is the size of a walk-in wardrobe, my oven is probably older than my great grandmother and my gas stovetop is about as temperamental as I am (more than a generous dollop). All I have is my food processor, a set of digital scales, a microplane, mandoline, spiralizer, a couple of saucepans and a non-stick frying pan—and really, that's all I need.

There are two kinds of cookbooks: coffee table books and plain old good cookbooks. The good-looking one usually sits in a designer living room, glossy and pristine and rarely looked through, while a good cookbook is dog-eared and spattered with sauce and remnants from the latest meal. I do hope you find the styling and photography of my food worthy of a spot in your living room, but I also hope that doesn't stop you covering it in flecks of whatever it is you are trying from *Bowl & Fork*. Most of all, I hope *Bowl & Fork* sparks creativity to get you in the kitchen and cooking.

Happy cooking.
Anna x

RISE AND SHINE

I'm not going to bore you with a list of reasons why breakfast is so important for your health (you already know that). Sweet or savory, eggs or muesli, everyone is quite particular about what they crave to break their overnight fast. As soon as I wake up, I'm thinking about what's in my breakfast bowl. I must admit that I'm a creature of habit and crave the same breakfast every day. While my husband will be offered a smorgasbord of options from Mum's Parmesan Scrambled Egg Bowl (pg 22) to Baked Shakshuka (baked egg dish) (pg 14), I will contentedly cuddle up with a cup of coffee and possibly the most humble of breakfast foods, rolled oats. In winter, it's a piping hot bowl of steel-cut oats and in summer, it's granola with yogurt and fruit or for a change, Strawberries and Cream Chia Pudding (pg 21). If I'm super organized, I like to make a big batch of Soaked Apple and Cinnamon Oats (pg 23) and put them in little containers, ready to take to work.

Weekday breakfasts are about nutrition and convenience while weekend breakfasts can feature a little indulgence, to celebrate the fact that you can stay in your pyjamas all day. Nothing gives me greater pleasure than getting in the kitchen before everyone wakes up, when there's no rush to get a meal on the table. With a cup of tea in hand, I start cooking a feast and slowly the smells of sautéing onions and garlic waft through the house, gently coaxing sleepy heads awake. Leisurely eating our breakfast on the balcony as we flick through the newspapers with nothing on the agenda, except for a late lunch.

BAKED SHAKSHUKA
with speck and fetta

Shakshuka is a deceptively simple baked egg dish that originated in North Africa. This interpretation strays from more traditional recipes with the addition of speck and fetta, which adds another dimension of flavor to the dish and the cheese softens into creamy, textural nuggets. It is served as it is cooked, in individual, small frying pans or ovenproof dishes. If you're feeding a crowd, rather than fiddling around with individual ramekins, use a large frying pan and serve it in the middle of the table for everyone to tuck in. This isn't strictly a breakfast meal either. You can enjoy it for lunch or dinner.

INGREDIENTS

2 tablespoons olive oil
1 tablespoon butter
3 garlic cloves, finely chopped
½ brown onion, peeled and finely diced
100 g (3½ oz) speck (or bacon), rind removed and finely chopped
1 teaspoon harissa paste
½ teaspoon ground cumin
1 tablespoon tomato paste

400 g (14 oz) tinned diced tomatoes
100 g (3½ oz) Danish fetta, roughly chopped
4 free-range eggs
4 slices sourdough, toasted

METHOD

1. Preheat oven to 200°C (400°F).
2. Add olive oil and butter to a large frying pan over a medium heat. Add garlic, onion and speck. Sauté until lightly golden and then add harissa paste, cumin, tomato paste and tomatoes. Reduce heat and, stirring occasionally, simmer for 5 minutes or until you have a thick sauce.
3. Divide mixture between 4 x 250 ml (8 fl oz) ovenproof pie dishes or small frying pans. Divide fetta between the four dishes, scattering the cheese evenly between each. Make a small well in the middle of the tomato mixture and gently crack an egg into each.
4. Transfer dishes to a baking tray and cook in the oven for 15–20 minutes or until egg white is cooked and yolk is still runny (if you prefer your egg yolks hard, cook for a further 5 minutes).
5. Serve as is with toasted sourdough on the side.

Harissa is a North African chili paste, available from most supermarkets, gourmet grocers and delicatessens.

CHUNKY CASHEW AND CRANBERRY GRANOLA

with maple cinnamon pears

I sent a little package of this granola to one of my best friends, Tallulah, and I received a text message a couple of days later: "It's seriously the best granola I've ever eaten". That's all I needed to get it in the book! When doing a kitchen cupboard clean up, granola is a great way to use up all those half packets of nuts, dried fruit and seeds. Cut back on the amount of maple syrup if you'd like to reduce the sweetness.

INGREDIENTS

300 g (10 oz) gluten free rolled oats
160 g (5½ oz) raw cashew nuts (roughly chopped, if you prefer)
125 ml (4 fl oz) apple juice
125 ml (4 fl oz) pure maple syrup (or honey)
60 ml (2 fl oz) coconut oil or olive oil
1 teaspoon vanilla extract
1 teaspoon sea salt
½ teaspoon ground cinnamon

100 g (3½ oz) dried cranberries

Maple cinnamon pears
2 pears (Beurre Bosc or Packham), halved, skin on and cored using a melon baller or spoon
1 tablespoon olive oil
2 teaspoons pure maple syrup
½ teaspoon cinnamon
½ teaspoon vanilla extract

METHOD

1. Preheat oven to 160°C (320°F).
2. Combine the oats and cashews in a large bowl.
3. In a medium saucepan, add the apple juice, maple syrup, coconut oil, vanilla extract, salt and cinnamon. Gently heat until salt is dissolved and coconut oil has melted.
4. Pour liquid over the oats and cashews and toss to coat. Spread the mixture evenly on a baking tray. Bake for 45–50 minutes or until lightly golden, stirring every 15 minutes to ensure the granola cooks evenly. (The key to a crunchy granola is cooking at a low temperature for a long time.)
5. Meanwhile, to bake the pears, mix olive oil, maple syrup, cinnamon and vanilla in a bowl. Add pears and toss to coat with mixture. Place pears, cut-side facing up, on a lined baking tray. Roast for 15 minutes or until lightly golden. Turn pears over and cook for a further 10–15 minutes or until golden and soft. Remove from oven and set aside.
6. Once granola is cooked, turn the oven off and leave to cool completely. Break up the granola into chunky clusters (or whatever size you prefer) and scatter with cranberries. The granola will keep for 2 weeks in an airtight container at room temperature.
7. Serve granola with milk of your choice, yogurt and half a pear. Reserve juice from the pears' roasting tray to drizzle over granola. In total, this makes about 640 g of muesli.

SMOKY CHORIZO BAKED BEANS

Who doesn't love baked beans? I admit, I have a soft spot for the tinned variety but this homemade version is certainly worth the extra effort. This recipe is a riff on American Boston baked beans, which are made with molasses. I use maple syrup and chorizo to give the beans that smoky-sweet flavor. If time is your friend, soak dried cannellini beans overnight and simmer for 1–1½ hours. Double the batch to freeze for a rainy day.

INGREDIENTS

3 tomatoes
1 tablespoon extra virgin olive oil
3 cloves garlic, peeled and finely chopped
1 brown onion, peeled and diced
150 g (5 oz) chorizo sausage, roughly diced
1 teaspoon smoked paprika

1 tablespoon tomato paste
1 tablespoon pure maple syrup
400 g (14 oz) tinned cannellini beans, drained and
 rinsed under cold water
sea salt and freshly ground pepper
2 tablespoons fresh flat-leaf parsley, roughly chopped

METHOD

1. Slice a cross on the top of your tomatoes before plunging into boiling water for 20 seconds. Using a slotted spoon, remove and drain. Peel tomato skin, discard and roughly dice.
2. Add oil to a saucepan over medium heat. Add garlic, onion and chorizo and sauté until onion is soft and translucent. Stir through smoked paprika, tomato paste, maple syrup, diced tomatoes and cannellini beans. Cover and simmer for 15–20 minutes. Season to taste.
3. Serve in a bowl, scattered with flat-leaf parsley, with toast on the side, if desired.

10-MINUTE PEANUT BUTTER GRANOLA

More often than I'd like to admit, breakfast is something thrown in a bowl, eaten at my desk at work. For those days, it's my 10-minute granola—rich, nutty, crunchy, sweet and salty. Originally it was just a simple granola with oats, honey and a sprinkle of cinnamon—then I added a spoonful (or three) of peanut butter. This recipe will delight any peanut-butter-and-honey-sandwich devotees.

INGREDIENTS

200 g (7 oz) gluten free rolled oats
100 g (3½ oz) almonds, roughly chopped
2 tablespoons olive oil (or coconut oil)
3 tablespoons honey (or pure maple syrup)
3 tablespoons crunchy peanut butter
½ teaspoon ground cinnamon
a sprinkle of sea salt

To serve
milk of your choice
gluten free Greek yogurt
1 passionfruit
seasonal fruit

METHOD

1. Place oats and roughly chopped almonds in a large frying pan. Dry roast on high heat for 5 minutes or until lightly golden, stirring often.
2. Pour over the oil and maple syrup. Continue stirring for a further 5 minutes, making sure the oats are well coated. Sprinkle with cinnamon and salt. Remove from the heat and allow to cool slightly.
3. Serve with milk, yogurt and drizzle with passionfruit pulp and a selection of seasonal fruit. The granola will keep for up to 2 weeks in an airtight container at room temperature.

STRAWBERRIES AND CREAM CHIA PUDDING

This chia pudding is the ultimate do-ahead-of-time, portable power breakfast. Chia seeds are high in omega-3 content, contain all nine essential amino acids and are packed full of antioxidants, calcium, magnesium and manganese. The tiny seeds expand to hold about 10 times their dry weight in liquid, swelling into gel-like balls to create this luxuriously creamy pudding. If you're partial to a little breakfast decadence or perhaps you're serving this for dessert, opt for double cream.

INGREDIENTS

Chia pudding
110 g (4 oz) black chia seeds
500 ml (16 fl oz) dairy, soy or almond milk
1 tablespoon pure maple syrup (or sweetener of
    choice: honey, agave nectar, brown rice syrup)
1 teaspoon cinnamon
½ teaspoon mixed spice
1 teaspoon vanilla extract

Toppings
500 g (1 lb) strawberries, fresh or frozen and thawed
100 g (3½ oz) gluten free Greek yogurt (double
    cream or coconut yogurt, if dairy intolerant)
goji berries (optional)
cacao nibs (optional)

METHOD

1. In a large bowl, whisk to combine chia seeds, almond milk, maple syrup (or your choice of sweetener), cinnamon, mixed spice and vanilla extract. Stir thoroughly, ensuring there are no clumps of chia (otherwise your pudding will be lumpy). Cover with plastic wrap and set aside for 15 minutes or, alternatively, place in the refrigerator overnight.
2. Meanwhile, place half the strawberries in a food processor and blend to a puree. Set aside in a bowl. Slice the remaining 250 g (9 oz) strawberries into quarters and mix with the strawberry puree.
3. Divide soaked chia pudding between bowls. Use a spoon to swirl through strawberry puree. Top with a generous dollop of your desired 'cream' and scatter with goji berries, cacao nibs and strawberries.

*Chia seeds are gluten free and suit a vegan diet. Chia pudding will last
in the refrigerator for several days.*

MUM'S PARMESAN SCRAMBLED EGG BOWL

with sautéed kale and avocado

Every time I visit my parents in the country, Mum begs me to whip up this for breakfast. I love the morning ritual of getting fresh eggs from the chicken coop, picking a few herbs from the veggie patch and having the time to sit and enjoy breakfast with the family. Roasting coaxes flavor from even out-of-season tomatoes while kale offers high doses of fiber, iron, vitamin K and antioxidants.

INGREDIENTS

Steamed quinoa
100 g (3½ oz) tricolor (red, black or white) quinoa, rinsed and drained
250 ml (8 fl oz) water

Roasted cherry tomatoes
150 g (5 oz) cherry tomatoes
1 tablespoon olive oil
sea salt and freshly ground pepper

Sautéed kale
1 tablespoon olive oil

1 clove garlic, thinly sliced
½ bunch of kale, rinsed and dried, ribs and stems removed, thinly sliced
squeeze lemon juice

Parmesan scrambled eggs
4 large free-range eggs, room temperature
100 ml (3½ oz) pure (single) cream
50 g (2 oz) fresh Parmesan, grated
1 tablespoon unsalted butter
6 scallions (spring onions), finely sliced
½ avocado, sliced

METHOD

1. Heat oven to 180°C (350°F).
2. To cook the quinoa, combine the quinoa and water in a saucepan. Bring to the boil. Cover, reduce heat and cook until the liquid has been absorbed and the quinoa is tender, about 15 minutes. Uncover, fluff the quinoa with a fork and set aside.
3. Place cherry tomatoes on a baking tray. Drizzle with olive oil, season and toss to coat. Bake for 15 minutes.
4. For the sautéed kale, heat oil in a frying pan over medium-high. Add garlic and sauté for 1 minute or until lightly golden. Add kale and continue to cook until tender. Squeeze some lemon juice over the kale and season with salt and pepper.
5. In a medium bowl, lightly whisk the eggs, cream, Parmesan and a pinch of salt. Set aside. Melt butter in a non-stick frying pan and add scallions. Pour in whisked egg mixture and let it sit, without stirring, for 20 seconds. Use a wooden spoon to lift and fold the eggs from the bottom of the pan (do not stir). Cook until the eggs are softly set and slightly runny in places, then remove from the heat and leave for a few seconds to finish cooking. Taste and adjust seasoning. Place kale and quinoa (if using) in the bottom of the bowl. Serve scrambled eggs to one side and roasted cherry tomatoes, and sliced avocado, to the other. Serve immediately.

SOAKED APPLE AND CINNAMON OATS

I love soaking oats—not only because of their creamy and chewy texture but soaking makes the oats easier for our bodies to digest and allows us to absorb more vitamins and minerals. I make a big batch of this on Sunday night and pre-portion individual servings to take to work each morning.

INGREDIENTS

100 g (3½ oz) gluten free rolled oats
500 ml (16 fl oz) milk of choice (I use unsweetened almond or soy milk)
1 red Pink Lady apple (or other variety), coarsely grated
60 g (2 oz) almond flakes

40 g (1½ oz) shredded coconut
1 tablespoon honey, warmed so it is runny
1 teaspoon ground cinnamon
1 tablespoon of gluten free Greek yogurt
handful of fresh berries

METHOD

1. The night before, mix the oats, milk, grated apple, almond, coconut, honey and cinnamon together in a bowl. Cover and soak overnight.
2. In the morning, divide the muesli between four bowls, top with yogurt and scatter with fresh berries or fruit of your choice.

CINNAMON STEEL-CUT OATS
with caramelized banana

Steel-cut oats aren't very popular in some places, however they're absolutely delicious so well worth finding. Made from whole oat groats—the "steel-cut" part of the name comes from how the groats are chopped into small, nubbly pieces. Steel-cut oats have a nuttier and earthier taste and have more bite (texture) than rolled oats. However, they do take longer to cook. The solution is to make a batch that will last a few days.

INGREDIENTS

200 g (7 oz) steel cut oats
500 ml (16 fl oz) water
250 ml (8 fl oz) dairy, soy or almond milk
½ teaspoon salt
1 teaspoon cinnamon
1 tablespoon butter
1 tablespoon sugar (more or less, depending on the ripeness of your bananas)
2 bananas, peeled and sliced in half lengthways
Greek yogurt

Optional toppings

chia seeds
shredded coconut
toasted buckwheat
almond butter
flax seeds
cacao nibs

METHOD

1. Pour the oats, water, milk and salt into a medium saucepan and bring to the boil. Watch carefully as the oats may bubble up quickly. Reduce the heat to low and bring the oats to a simmer. Cook, uncovered, stirring occasionally, for 15-20 minutes or until oats are just cooked.
2. Meanwhile, melt the butter and sugar in a medium frying pan. Add the banana halves and cook until lightly golden and caramelized.
3. Once oats are cooked, stir through cinnamon and divide between four bowls.
4. Arrange caramelized banana on top of oats, scatter with optional toppings (if desired) and serve with a dash more milk or a dollop of Greek yogurt.

*This will keep well in the refrigerator. Add a dash more milk and reheat
small portions gently on the stove or in the microwave.*

SNACKS AND STARTERS

Snacking is part of my DNA. I graze constantly, whether it's a handful of granola, hummus, a piece of fruit or a small bowl of soup, I feel deprived if I don't have something to tide me over between 'proper' meals. In saying that, I never want a snack to spoil my appetite for the next meal so I tend to lean towards balanced snacks that are easy on the waistline. Roasted Garlic Hummus (pg 31) is a favorite and it is great to bulk up salads or as a mid-afternoon pick me up. I've found that Honey Glazed Chicken and Edamame Meatballs (pg 42) is a crowd pleaser and is equally good as a light lunch, snack or dinner party starter. If you're the kind of person who needs an afternoon sugar hit, try the Not Naughty But Nice Salted Caramel Popcorn (pg 34); it's sweet, salty and crunchy. Warning: they're addictive.

Unlike snacks, my dinner party starters are all about arousing taste buds. Laotian Duck Larb (pg 36) and Gruyere, Parmesan and Ricotta Zucchini Flowers (pg 40) aren't dishes you'll eat everyday (especially since zucchini flowers are seasonal) but they'll certainly impress guests. The Fritto Misto (pg 39) makes a beautiful starter on a hot, summer's day, especially when served with the Pickled Fennel Salad, which is a standout dish in its own right. On the other hand, dishes such as the Son-In-Law Eggs (pg 35), Caramelized Onion, Silverbeet and Yogurt Dip (pg 29) or Moroccan Spiced Cauliflower Soup (pg 33) are nutritious and healthy options that you can enjoy regularly.

RED LENTIL DHAL
with coconut roti

In India, dhal (dal) means dried legume and is traditionally a thick puree, stew or soup, served with rice and chapati. Here, I've served it as a dip however I sometimes add more stock to make a soup and then perk it up with some chunks of poached salmon. If you're feeling ambitious, definitely give the coconut roti a try—trust me, you won't regret the extra effort. Red lentils are perfect for weeknights because they don't require soaking and cook a lot quicker than any other variety of legumes.

INGREDIENTS
Dhal
200 g (7 oz) dried red lentils
1 tablespoon olive oil
1 small brown onion, peeled and finely diced
3 cloves garlic, finely diced
1cm fresh ginger, finely grated
1 teaspoon ground cumin
1 teaspoon garam masala
½ teaspoon ground turmeric
¼ teaspoon chili powder
750 ml (1½ pints) quality chicken or vegetable stock

1 teaspoon sea salt
2 tablespoons fresh cilantro (coriander), finely
   chopped

Coconut roti
500 g (1 lb) all purpose (plain) flour
100 g (3½ oz) desiccated coconut
1 teaspoon sea salt
370 ml (12 fl oz) warm water
100 ml (3 fl oz) rice bran oil

METHOD
1. Place lentils in a bowl and wash a few times with cold water. Cover lentils with water and remove any that float. Drain lentils in a colander and set aside.
2. Heat oil in a saucepan over medium-high. Add onion, garlic and ginger and sauté until lightly golden, about 2 minutes. Add drained lentils, cumin, garam masala, turmeric and chili powder. Cook, stirring until the lentils are coated. Stir through the stock. Reduce heat and simmer uncovered for 40 minutes, stirring occasionally. Set aside to cool slightly for 10 minutes.
3. Meanwhile, to make the coconut roti, place the flour, coconut and salt in a large bowl. Add the water a little at a time. Use your hands to mix to form a smooth dough. Divide the dough into 12 balls. Place in a bowl and set aside until ready to cook.
4. When the dhal is almost ready, take a ball of dough and, using the palm of your hand, spread to form a thin disc, about 10 cm (½ inch) in diameter and 5 cm (1/4 inch) thick. Keep uncooked dough covered with a damp tea towel to stop the dough from drying out.
5. Heat a small amount of the oil in a frying pan over high heat. Add the roti and cook until golden, then flip and cook the other side until lightly golden. Remove from the pan and drain on absorbent paper. Cover with foil. Repeat with the remaining dough until you have cooked all the roti. Serve dhal scattered with cilantro and warm coconut roti.

CARAMELIZED ONION, SILVERBEET AND YOGURT DIP

Ah, caramelized onions, the smell wafting through the house and the tender, sweet and savory flavors. There are few things in the world that make me wiggle my toes with glee. You can't rush caramelized onions. Be patient and move each onion strand around the pan until they reach that gorgeous golden color. I'm always on the search for snacks that are delicious and healthy. This is so yum, you won't even think that you're being good!

INGREDIENTS

2 tablespoons extra virgin olive oil
2 brown onions, peeled and sliced lengthways
100 g (3½ oz) swiss chard (silverbeet), thick middle
    stalks removed
150 g (5 oz) gluten free natural yogurt
½ teaspoon onion powder
½ garlic clove, finely grated on a microplane
sea salt and freshly ground pepper

METHOD

1. Heat oil in a large frying pan or saucepan to medium-low. Add onions and sauté, stirring regularly until golden and caramelized, about 20 minutes. Set aside to cool.
2. Wash swiss chard and place in a saucepan. Without adding any water, cover and heat to medium. Cook until it has completely wilted and chop roughly. Allow to cool.
3. In a serving bowl, combine swiss chard, yogurt, onion powder and garlic. Stir through three-quarters of the caramelized onions. Taste and season accordingly.
4. Scatter with remaining caramelized onions and serve with Salt and Pepper Lavosh (pg 32) or a selection of sliced baby vegetables (carrots, cucumbers, celery, fennel).

A tip for all those diehard caramelized onion lovers like me, you can actually freeze them for a few months to whip out for a quick pissaladière tart or for this dip.

CHARRED CORN AND GOAT'S CHEESE GUACAMOLE

Perked up with salty goat's cheese and charred corn kernels, this chunky avocado dip becomes something quite brilliant. The quality of the avocado is crucial so select one that is firm but still ripe. I always buy a few (just in case the first one isn't perfect). If your avocado is under-ripe, place it in a paper bag with a banana to speed up the ripening process.

INGREDIENTS

1 x 150 g (5 oz) ear of corn
2 tablespoons extra virgin olive oil
salt and freshly ground pepper
1 garlic clove, finely grated on a microplane
2 ripe avocados
1 long red chili, seeds removed, finely chopped

2 tablespoons fresh lime juice
1 teaspoon ground cumin
40 g (1½ oz) goat's cheese (or fetta), crumbled
2 tablespoons fresh cilantro (coriander), finely
  chopped

METHOD

1. Remove the outer husk from the corn and peel away the silk (white string).
2. Heat a hot grill, barbecue or griddle pan to medium-high. Rub oil over the corn and place directly onto the heat. Cook for 6–10 minutes turning every few minutes, until evenly charred. Allow to cool and then stand upright on its base and use a sharp knife to shave off the charred kernels.
3. Cut the avocadoes in half, remove the pits (seeds). Score both ways and then scoop out the flesh with a spoon and place in a large bowl. Combine all the remaining ingredients in a bowl. Using the back of a fork, mash to combine. Taste and season with salt and pepper. Serve with corn chips or just eat with a fork.

*If you make guacamole ahead of time, simply pour a little water on the
surface to stop the avocado turning brown. Pour the water off before
you serve. I promise it won't get soggy.*

ROASTED GARLIC HUMMUS

Pumpkin hummus, beetroot hummus, kale hummus, tzatzummus (hummus-tzatziki hybrid), I've cooked them all, so strong is my love for the humble chickpea dip. This has to be my fave. For ease, I have used canned chickpeas. You'll find dried chickpeas, soaked overnight and cooked, make the hummus a lot creamier.

INGREDIENTS

1 head of garlic, whole
½ tablespoon olive oil
1 x 400 g (14 oz) tinned chickpeas, drained
2 tablespoons hulled tahini
3 tablespoons lemon juice
2 tablespoons extra virgin olive oil

1 teaspoon ground cumin
½ teaspoon sumac
½ teaspoon sea salt
2 tablespoons water
1 tablespoon fresh flat-leaf parsley, roughly chopped

METHOD

1. Preheat oven to 180°C (350°F).
2. Coat garlic head with olive oil and wrap in foil. Roast in the oven for 1 hour. Remove and allow to cool. Using your fingers, squeeze the soft, roasted garlic out of each clove and place in the food processor.
3. Drain the chickpeas, rinse well and transfer to the food processor with the garlic. Add the remaining ingredients and blend until smooth. If the consistency is too thick, add a couple of tablespoons of water. Tip into a bowl and, when ready to serve, drizzle with olive oil and scatter with sumac and flat-leaf parsley.
4. Serve with Salt and Pepper Lavosh (pg 32).

Sumac is used in a lot of Middle Eastern cooking and can be bought at any good grocer or delicatessen. Hummus can be refrigerated for up to 5 days.

SALT AND PEPPER LAVOSH

Lavosh is a crunchy Middle Eastern cracker that makes a great addition to any cheeseboard. I'm always shocked at how much lavosh costs in gourmet grocers, especially when it's so easy to make at home. I prefer just salt and pepper, however you can add any ground spices, sesame seeds or even Parmesan.

INGREDIENTS

270 g (9½ oz) all purpose (plain) flour
100 g (3½ oz) whole wheat (wholemeal) flour
125 ml (4 fl oz) extra virgin olive oil

250 ml (8 fl oz) water
3 teaspoons sea salt (I use pink Himalayan salt)
2 teaspoons freshly ground black pepper

METHOD

1. Preheat oven to 180°C (350°F).
2. In a large bowl, stir to combine both flours.
3. In a separate bowl, combine the oil and water and then slowly add to the combined flour mixture. Knead to form a soft, moist dough.
4. Divide dough into 4 separate balls. Using a wooden rolling pin, roll each ball onto a piece of baking (parchment) paper into a rectangle about 30 cm (12 inch) x 20 cm (8 inch). Make sure it is as thin as possible, about 2 mm (1/10 inch). It's important the dough is rolled out paper thin, so that you end up with crisp crackers.
5. Place onto 4 oven trays (or repeat using the same tray) and generously sprinkle with sea salt and black pepper. Bake until lightly golden, about 15 minutes. Set aside to cool, then break into rough shards, crackers or any shape you desire.

MOROCCAN SPICED CAULIFLOWER SOUP WITH CRISP PANCETTA

This is one of those utterly soul-satisfying soups. From making 'rice' to roasting, frying, steaming and even creating pizza crusts, there seems to be no limit to the culinary potential of cauliflower. The soup is creamy enough on its own but for a little extra indulgence, add a dollop of crème fraîche or cream to serve. The addition of pancetta isn't crucial but I had to get my husband to try it somehow!

INGREDIENTS

2 tablespoons extra virgin olive oil
1 brown onion, peeled and finely diced
4 cloves garlic, finely chopped
1 teaspoon ground cinnamon
2 teaspoons ground cumin
1 teaspoon ground coriander
½ teaspoon ground chili

1 large cauliflower (about 1 kg/2 lb), trimmed and
   broken into small florets
1 L (1¾ pint) Homemade Chicken Stock (pg 180) or
   good quality store-bought stock
120 g (4 oz) pancetta (Italian bacon)
sea salt and freshly ground pepper
1 tablespoon fresh chives, roughly chopped

METHOD

1. Preheat oven to 180°C (350°F).
2. Add olive oil to a large frying pan over medium heat. Add onion, stirring occasionally, until softened and translucent. Stir through garlic and cook for a further minute. Add the cinnamon, cumin, coriander and chili and cook until fragrant, about a minute.
3. Add cauliflower and chicken stock. If you like a runnier soup, add 125 ml (4 fl oz) more stock at this point. Cover and cook until the cauliflower is tender, about 20 minutes.
4. Meanwhile, place the pancetta on a large baking tray. Bake in oven for 8–10 minutes or until crisp. Set aside to cool slightly. Break into coarse shards.
5. Using a blender or food processor, puree the soup until smooth. Taste and adjust seasoning, as required remembering that the pancetta is quite salty. Before serving, return soup to heat and warm.
6. Ladle into warmed bowls and scatter with crispy pancetta and chives.

*The soup can be made ahead of time, so this makes a fantastic midweek
winter meal.*

NOT NAUGHTY BUT NICE SALTED CARAMEL POPCORN

For the kid in us all, this sticky, salty, sweet and crunchy popcorn is perfect for winter nights watching back-to-back episodes of the latest TV series you're hooked on. This is not a hard set caramel so be prepared for some serious finger-lickin'. If you're not terribly good at sharing food, serve in individual bowls or, better yet, double the batch.

INGREDIENTS
1 tablespoon olive oil
100 g (3½ oz) popping corn
4 tablespoons pure maple syrup
1 teaspoon pure vanilla extract
2 teaspoons sea salt (or more)

METHOD
1. To pop the corn, pour the oil into a large, heavy-based saucepan with a lid. Turn the heat up to medium and add the corn kernels. Cover and give the pot a good shake to evenly coat the corn in oil. Continue to cook over medium heat for about 30 seconds and then open the lid slightly, to allow the steam to escape. Continue to cook, shaking occasionally until the popping stops, about 2 minutes. Remove from the heat and pour onto a tray lined with baking (parchment) paper. Discard any un-popped corn kernels left in the bottom of the saucepan.
2. Meanwhile, make the salted caramel sauce. In a small saucepan, bring the maple syrup, vanilla and sea salt to a boil, whisking constantly. Reduce heat and cook for a further 1 minute. Remove from the heat.
3. Arrange popcorn in a single layer and then drizzle the salted caramel sauce over the popcorn and toss to combine. Add more salt if desired and serve immediately.

SON-IN-LAW EGGS
with tamarind dressing

I just adore this recipe; a bowl of soft-boiled eggs, all dressed up with a sweet-and-sour tamarind dressing. Traditionally, son-in-law eggs are fried and while that's delicious, it's not something you want to cook and eat every day. This is my healthier yet equally delicious soft-boiled egg version.

INGREDIENTS

Tamarind dressing

1 tablespoon rice bran oil
6 garlic cloves, finely chopped
½ large Spanish onion, peeled and finely diced
3 tablespoons tamarind puree (store-bought)
2 tablespoons tamari
1 tablespoon pure maple syrup
1 tablespoon gluten free fish sauce

Soft-boiled eggs

6–8 free-range eggs, at room temperature
2 scallions (spring onions), white part only, finely chopped
1 tablespoon fresh cilantro (coriander), roughly chopped
1 tablespoon fresh mint, roughly chopped
1 long red chili, deseeded and sliced

METHOD

1. Heat a small saucepan with oil to medium-high. Add garlic and Spanish onion and cook until lightly golden and caramelized. Add the tamarind puree, tamari, maple syrup and fish sauce and stir through. Cook until combined, about 1 minute. Take off the heat and set aside to cool slightly.
2. Meanwhile, bring a saucepan of water with a generous pinch of sea salt to the boil. Gently submerge eggs and cook for exactly 6 minutes. Drain and run under cold water (if you prefer hard-boiled eggs, cook for 7–8 minutes). Once cool enough to handle, remove shell and slice in half.
3. Arrange in a bowl or on a serving platter. Top with a spoonful of thick tamarind dressing and scatter with scallions, coriander, mint and chili.

*Tamarind puree can be bought in supermarkets however if using
tamarind pulp with seeds, double the quantity of tamarind and mix with
hot water, squeezing to dissolve the pulp (separate and discard seeds).*

LAOTIAN DUCK LARB

Crunching through a layer of fresh greens and reaching a mix of salty cashews, rich duck slices, zingy lemongrass and kaffir lime is a universally satisfying experience. Traditionally, larb is a minced meat salad, widely regarded as the national dish of Laos. The dressing is key so taste and adjust accordingly. It must be a balance of sweet, sour, salty and bitter.

INGREDIENTS

Duck larb

2 x 250 g (9 oz) duck breasts, skin on

2 tablespoons peanut oil

3 scallions (spring onions), white part, finely sliced

1 tablespoon lemongrass, white part only, finely sliced

4 kaffir lime leaves, middle vein removed and finely sliced

1 long fresh chili, deseeded and finely chopped

½ bunch mint, roughly chopped

½ bunch cilantro (coriander), roughly chopped

Dressing

60 ml (2 fl oz) lime juice, freshly squeezed

2 tablespoons gluten free fish sauce

1½ tablespoons light palm sugar, grated

To serve

2 tablespoons cashews, unsalted and roasted

Baby cos leaves

METHOD

1. Preheat oven to 180°C (350°F).
2. Using a sharp knife, score the skin of the duck in a criss-cross pattern, taking care not to cut into the flesh. Rub sea salt and black pepper into the skin.
3. Add peanut oil to a large frying pan over medium heat. Add the duck breasts, skin-side down, and cook for 8–9 minutes or until most of the fat has rendered and the skin is crisp. Flip the duck breast over and cook for 1–2 minutes. Transfer to a baking tray and cook in pre-heated oven for 8 minutes. Reserve any duck fat in the pan to make Sweet Potato Wedges (pg 77). Remove duck from oven and allow to rest, skin side up, for at least 5 minutes.
4. Meanwhile, prepare the dressing by combining the lime juice, fish sauce and palm sugar in a small bowl. Whisk until the palm sugar is dissolved.
5. Cut the duck breasts into 5 mm (¼ inch) thick slices. Place duck in a large bowl, add scallions, lemongrass, sliced kaffir lime leaves, chili and herbs. Pour over the dressing and toss to combine. Scatter with roughly chopped cashews.
6. Cut off the hard white end of the baby cos lettuce with scissors to form 8 cups. There's no need to use bowls for this one—the baby cos cups are all you need!
7. Serve immediately as is or with Steamed Jasmine Rice (pg 185) or vermicelli noodles to make a more substantial meal.

Duck fat will keep for days in the refrigerator or months frozen. The duck can easily be replaced with pork or chicken mince.

FRITTO MISTO
with pickled fennel salad

I find the combination of fried seafood with this sweet and salty pickled fennel salad so delightfully addictive, especially when served with a generous dollop of Whole Egg Mayonnaise.

INGREDIENTS

Pickled fennel salad
½ baby fennel bulb, about 200 g (7 oz), halved and
   fronds reserved
4 tablespoons white wine vinegar
2 tablespoons sugar
2 teaspoons salt
60 g (2 oz) wild rocket (arugula)
1 tablespoon extra virgin olive oil
sea salt and freshly ground black pepper

Batter
200 g (7 oz) all purpose (plain) flour

1 teaspoon bicarbonate of soda
¼ teaspoon salt
400 ml (14 fl oz) iced water

Fritto misto
4 medium green shrimp (prawns), peeled and
   de-veined
8 baby whiting fillets
4 baby squid, cleaned and beak removed, sliced into
   rings and tentacles halved
vegetable oil, to deep or shallow-fry
1 lemon, cut into wedges

METHOD

1. Use a mandoline or sharp knife to shave the fennel into a medium, heatproof bowl. Cut off the fronds, finely chop and set aside.
2. Place vinegar, sugar and salt in a small saucepan and bring to the boil. Cook, stirring occasionally, until the sugar dissolves. Pour this pickling liquid over the sliced fennel and cover with plastic wrap. Set aside for at least 20 minutes or up to 12 hours to pickle. Drain sliced fennel, reserving 1–2 tablespoons of the pickling liquid.
3. Place drained fennel, rocket and fennel fronds in a bowl. Add extra virgin olive oil and 1-2 tablespoons of reserved pickling liquid and toss to combine. Taste and season.
4. To make the fritto misto, place plain flour, bicarbonate of soda and salt in a medium bowl. Add 400 ml (14 fl oz) iced water and gently mix with a fork until just combined.
5. Fill a deep fryer or large saucepan one-third full with vegetable oil. Heat deep fryer to 180°C (350°F). If using a saucepan, heat to medium-high or until a cube of bread turns golden in 10 seconds.
6. For the seafood, cook the shrimp, whiting and squid separately as they cook at different rates. Start with the shrimp. Dip in batter and then shake off any excess batter. Gently drop into oil and fry until crisp and golden, about 2–3 minutes. Remove with a slotted spoon and drain on paper towel. Season immediately. Repeat for the whiting and then the squid.
7. Divide salad between serving bowls and top with fried seafood (fritto misto). Serve with Whole Egg Mayonnaise (pg 181) and lemon wedges on the side.

GRUYERE, PARMESAN AND RICOTTA ZUCCHINI FLOWERS

Nothing beats these crisp, cheese-stuffed zucchini flowers. They're the perfect dinner party starter or as a light lunch. If you can't get gruyere, you can stuff them with just ricotta and a few herbs.

INGREDIENTS

Batter
200 g (7 oz) all purpose (plain) flour
300 ml (10½ fl oz) soda water
vegetable oil

Zucchini flowers
12 zucchini flowers, baby zucchini attached
150 g (5 oz) Parmesan, grated
150 g (5 oz) Homemade Ricotta (pg 181) or
    store-bought

150 g (5 oz) gruyere, grated
2–3 sprigs fresh thyme, finely chopped
¼ cup flat-leaf parsley, finely chopped
100 g (3½ oz) baby rocket (arugula)
2 tablespoons extra virgin olive oil
1 lemon, juiced
sea salt and freshly ground pepper
basil leaves
Salsa Verde, (pg 101), optional

METHOD

1. Combine flour and soda water in a bowl and stir to form a rough, lumpy mixture; don't work the batter too much. Set aside to rest.
2. To make the filling, place Parmesan, ricotta and gruyere in a bowl. Add thyme and flat-leaf parsley and season with salt and freshly ground pepper.
3. Gently pull apart the zucchini petals and remove stamen or pistil (if you haven't already). Peel back the petals and, using scissors, snip off the stamen or pistil.
4. Place a heaped teaspoon of cheese mixture in each zucchini flower, twisting tips of petals to seal. Place on a tray until ready to cook. You may have leftover stuffing mixture. Think of it as chef's treat—I always end up nibbling more than my fair share!
5. Place rocket, extra virgin olive oil, lemon juice, salt and pepper in bowl. Using your hands, toss until all the leaves are dressed.
6. Fill a deep fryer all the way or a large saucepan one-third full with vegetable oil and heat to 180°C (350°F). If using a saucepan, heat to medium-high or until a cube of bread turns golden in 10 seconds.
7. Dip zucchini flowers in batter to coat. Gently shake to remove excess batter and fry, in batches, turning occasionally, until golden, about 2–3 minutes. Drain on absorbent paper and season with salt. Repeat with remaining zucchini flowers.
8. Place a handful of rocket in a bowl. Top with 2–3 zucchini flowers, lemon wedges and Salsa Verde (if using). Garnish with basil leaves. Serve immediately.

HONEY-GLAZED CHICKEN AND EDAMAME MEATBALLS

with wasabi and jalapeño guacamole

This mightn't be the prettiest dish but it's absolutely delicious and will please kids and adults alike. The addition of wasabi to the guacamole gives this recipe a good kick but if you're feeding little ones, just tone the heat back or omit. Edamame, unripened green soybeans, are one of the few plant-based foods that provide a complete protein. They are available frozen from most supermarkets.

INGREDIENTS

250 g (9 oz) frozen edamame beans
600 g (1 lb 5 oz) lean chicken mince
½ brown onion, peeled and finely diced
2 garlic cloves, finely grated on a microplane
1 cm ginger, finely grated on a microplane
1 egg, lightly beaten
½ teaspoon sea salt

Glaze

4 tablespoons tamari
4 tablespoons mirin
2 tablespoons honey

Wasabi and jalapeño guacamole

2 ripe avocados
2 jalapeños, finely chopped
3 tablespoons fresh lime juice
1 teaspoon wasabi paste
1 teaspoon tamari
2 tablespoons fresh cilantro (coriander), roughly chopped
¼ teaspoon sea salt and freshly ground pepper

METHOD

1. Preheat oven to 180°C (350°F).
2. Run the frozen edamame under water to thaw. Push the beans out of the pods and pat dry. This should yield about 125 g (4 oz) edamame beans. Place the beans, chicken mince, onion, garlic, ginger, egg and salt in a food processor. Blend until just combined. Shape mixture into balls, about 1 tablespoon in size. Place on a roasting tray lined with baking (parchment) paper and store in the refrigerator until ready to cook.
3. Meanwhile, to make the glaze, combine the tamari, mirin and honey in a small saucepan. Cook, stirring constantly, for 5 minutes or until reduced to a glaze consistency. Set aside to cool completely.
4. To make the wasabi guacamole, cut the avocadoes in half, remove pits, score both ways and then scoop out the flesh with a spoon. Place in a large bowl. Add the remaining guacamole ingredients and, using the back of a fork, mash to combine.
5. Remove patties from the refrigerator and brush with glaze. Transfer to the oven and, basting every 5 minutes, cook for 15 minutes or until lightly golden.
6. Serve chicken balls on top of guacamole and scatter with the remaining cilantro.

TEA SMOKED SALMON

In ancient cooking, smoking was originally a technique to preserve food but here we use a hot smoking method to add another flavor dimension to the salmon. Salmon is the perfect protein to smoke because of its high oil content keeps the salmon from drying out. Whether you're cold or hot-smoking, the process involves fire and smoke so, if possible, cook outdoors. Make sure you serve this dish accompanied with the Cucumber, Avocado, Mint and Watercress Salad (pg 135)—it's the perfect match.

INGREDIENTS

Marinated salmon

1 garlic clove, peeled and grated on a microplane
1 cm (½ inch) fresh ginger, grated on a microplane
¼ teaspoon five spice
1 tablespoon olive oil
2 teaspoons tamari
1 teaspoon brown sugar
¼ orange, juice
½ teaspoon orange zest
4 x 160 g (5½ oz) salmon fillets, skin removed, pin-boned

Tea smoking mix

3 tablespoons rice
2 tablespoons loose Earl Grey tea leaves or any black or green tea variety (each type of tea will produce a different taste)
2 tablespoons brown sugar
2 star anise, broken
2 dry red chilies, roughly chopped

METHOD

1. To make the marinade, combine all the ingredients in a shallow bowl, large enough to fit the 4 salmon fillets. Place the salmon fillets in the bowl and coat with marinade. Cover with cling wrap and transfer to the refrigerator until ready to smoke.
2. To prepare for smoking, you will need a wok and a bamboo steamer basket that fits inside your wok (if you don't have a steam basket, you can use wire rack—just make sure that it fits in the wok). Line the wok with 4 layers of foil. In a small bowl, mix smoking ingredients together and pour into the base of the wok, spreading the mixture across the bottom of the foil. Place the bamboo steamer or wire rack over the smoking mixture, so it sits above but is not directly touching. (You want space for the smoke to circulate).
3. Remove salmon from the marinade and shake off the excess liquid. Place salmon in the bamboo steamer, so that the pieces aren't touching each other or the edges of the wok. Tightly cover the entire wok (including the bamboo steamer) with foil to secure.
4. Place wok on high heat for 4–5 minutes or until you begin to see little puffs of smoke. You may have to open the foil a little to check if it is smoking. Once you see smoke, turn the heat down to medium for a further 5 minutes. To serve, break the still-warm salmon into chunks using your hands.
5. Place equal amounts of the Cucumber, Acocado, Mint and Watercress Salad (pg 135) between the bowls. Top with salmon chunks and serve.

RICE BOWLS

For me, rice might just be the ultimate comfort food. More nights than I'd like to admit, I throw together whatever's left in my refrigerator and construct a hodgepodge rice bowl. It's a meal that offers variety, versatility and it's easy to prepare and nourishing. Plus, it's perfect for cooking for one.

Rice is one of those indispensable pantry staples. There are so many varieties that you could never become bored. Widely available rices include long grain, jasmine, basmati and arborio varieties. Other less familiar rices are forbidden rice, often called black rice (see Teriyaki Salmon, pg 52), brown rice, wild rice and red rice or spiced rice dishes—such as the Indian Spiced Pilau (pg 186) and Steamed Coconut and Kaffir Lime Rice (pg 184) in the Pantry Essentials. It's tough to beat a bowl of freshly cooked rice scooped straight from the saucepan, the steam wafting into the air as you separate the tiny grains with a fork. I tend to use whole grain rice varieties as they're a bit more rustic, hearty and nutritionally sound.

Rice can be the star of the dish, like Sushi Roll In a Bowl (pg 57), or a vessel to soak up the aromatic coconut curry flavors in Seafood Choo Chee Curry (pg 58). There are also so many different methods for cooking rice; from washing or toasting the rice, adding salt when steaming, to steam covered or uncovered—everyone has their own way. Regardless of the method, one ancient Indian proverb rings true for them all: "Perfectly cooked rice grains are like brothers, close, yet separate, and definitely not stuck together."

KOREAN BEEF BIBIMBAP

What I love about this traditional Korean dish is the endless variations. I have used beef mince however you can char-grill scotch fillet or rib eye to slice on top or mix and match the vegetable dishes.

INGREDIENTS

Sesame vinaigrette
2 tablespoons rice wine vinegar
1 tablespoon sesame oil

Vegetables
2 Lebanese cucumbers, thinly sliced lengthways
½ teaspoon sea salt
1 teaspoon sesame oil
2 small carrots, peeled, chopped into thin matchsticks
100 g (3½ oz) bean sprouts, trimmed
80 g (3 oz) baby spinach

Beef bowl
2 tablespoons peanut oil or any vegetable oil
2 garlic cloves, peeled and finely chopped
1 cm (½ inch) fresh ginger, finely grated

750 g (1 lb 8 oz) lean beef mince
4 tablespoons tamari (or light soy sauce)
1 tablespoon brown sugar
2 tablespoons sake or dry sherry

To serve
4 free-range eggs
1 tablespoon peanut oil or any vegetable oil
1 tablespoon gochujang (Korean chili paste)
1 tablespoon white sesame seeds, roasted
2 sheets of nori, shredded
4 scallions (spring onions), thinly sliced
Steamed Sushi Rice (pg 187)

METHOD

1. Start by preparing the sesame vinaigrette. Combine the rice vinegar and sesame oil in a small bowl. Whisk to combine.
2. Toss the cucumber with ½ teaspoon salt (or to taste) and place in a colander. Set over a bowl to drain for 15–20 minutes. Rinse and squeeze dry. Place in a bowl and toss with 2 teaspoons of the sesame vinaigrette. Set aside.
3. Heat a non-stick frying pan to high and stir-fry carrot with 2 teaspoons sesame vinaigrette. Place in a bowl and set aside. Next, stir-fry bean sprouts with another 2 teaspoons sesame vinaigrette. Place in a bowl and set aside.
4. In a saucepan of boiling water, blanch baby spinach to wilt, then drain and place in a small bowl. Toss with 2 teaspoons of sesame vinaigrette and set aside.
5. Next, add beef and peanut oil to a large frying pan and cook over high heat. Add the garlic, ginger and beef mince. Cook until lightly golden and crisp. Reduce heat and stir through the tamari, brown sugar and sake. Cook for a further 2 minutes.
6. In a separate non-stick frying pan, heat oil to medium-high and fry eggs until the whites are just set and yolks are still runny.
7. Divide steamed rice between warm bowls. Surround with beef and vegetables, each ingredient in its own little pile. Place a fried egg and a teaspoon of kochujang (per person) on top of the rice and garnish with sesame seeds, shredded nori and scallions.

YAKITORI CHICKEN SKEWERS
with fragrant rice salad

Lathered in a thick soy sauce and charred until caramelized, these chicken skewers are plain genius. Shichimi togarashi is a Japanese spice blend that can be found in selected supermarkets and Asian food stores. If unavailable, use chili powder.

INGREDIENTS

3 tablespoons tamari

2 tablespoons pure maple syrup

1 tablespoon sake (Japanese rice wine)

1 tablespoon mirin (sweet rice wine or sweet sherry)

1 cm (½ inch) ginger, finely grated

2 garlic cloves, peeled and finely grated

750 g (1 lb 8 oz) chicken thigh fillets, deboned, skin removed, cut into 4 cm (1½ inch) pieces

4 scallions (spring onions) or baby leeks, white andlight green parts only, cut into 3 cm (1¼ inch) pieces

16 short bamboo skewers, soaked in water for 30 minutes

shichimi togarashi (optional)

Fragrant rice salad

100 g (3½ oz) jasmine rice

½ teaspoon sea salt

125 ml (4¼ fl oz) cold water

125 ml (4 fl oz) rice wine vinegar

60 g (2 oz) sugar

500 g (1 lb) Chinese cabbage (wombok), finely shredded

½ Spanish onion, peeled and finely sliced lengthwise

2 carrot, peeled and grated or sliced into noodles using a mandoline or spiralizer

1 tablespoon tamari (or light soy sauce)

1 teaspoon sesame oil

½ bunch cilantro (coriander), roughly chopped

½ bunch mint, roughly chopped

METHOD

1. To make yakitori marinade, place tamari, maple syrup, sake, mirin, ginger and garlic in medium bowl and stir until combined. Add chicken, cover and refrigerate for 30 minutes or overnight.
2. To make the fragrant rice salad, start by steaming the rice. Place the rice and salt in a medium saucepan with cold water. Bring to the boil, reduce heat, cover and cook for 10–12 minutes or until all the water has been absorbed and the rice is cooked. Uncover and fluff the rice with a fork. Set aside to cool.
3. Combine vinegar and sugar in a saucepan over medium heat. Stir until sugar dissolves, reduce heat and simmer uncovered for 5 minutes or until the liquid has reduced slightly.
4. Add cabbage, onion and carrot to a large bowl. Pour warm vinegar over salad and cover with plastic wrap. Set aside to cool.
5. Thread chicken pieces and spring onion, lengthwise and alternately, onto soaked skewers. Heat a chargrill pan or barbecue to medium-high. Add skewers in batches, turning and basting with reserved marinade occasionally. Cook for 4 minutes or until just cooked through.
6. Once Chinese cabbage is cool, stir through tamari, sesame oil, coriander, mint and steamed jasmine rice. Toss to combine.
7. Divide fragrant rice salad between bowls. Add 2 skewers per bowl and sprinkle with shichimi togarashi.

SKINNY GIRL CAULIFLOWER RICE

When my husband is working late and I want a healthy (but tasty) meal for one, this is my go-to dish. Cauliflower 'rice' is all the rage but, by itself, it's not very satisfying. I've bulked it up with shrimp, an egg, a good kick of chili and some fresh herbs. This dish can use up any leftover bits and bobs from the refrigerator and any veggies that are on their last limbs.

INGREDIENTS

1 cauliflower (about 1 kg/2 lb), cut into florets
2 tablespoons rice bran oil (or any neutral oil)
4 free-range eggs, lightly beaten
1 brown onion, peeled and finely diced
4 garlic cloves, peeled and finely chopped
1 cm (½ inch) fresh ginger, finely grated
750 g (1 lb 8 oz) green shrimp (prawns), cleaned, shelled and deveined

1 long red chili, de-seeded and thinly sliced
2 tablespoons tamari
2 teaspoons gluten free fish sauce
1 teaspoon sesame oil
sea salt and freshly ground pepper
4 scallions (spring onions), finely chopped
2 tablespoons fresh cilantro (coriander), chopped
1 tablespoon fresh mint, roughly chopped

METHOD

1. Place the cauliflower in a microwave dish and cook on high for about 4 minutes. Do not add any water. Place in a food processor and pulse until it resembles the texture of rice.
2. Heat half the oil a wok or frying pan until just smoking. Add the eggs and move them around the wok gently until just set. Transfer the eggs to a cutting board and roughly chop into pieces.
3. Heat the remaining oil (1 tablespoon) in the same wok or frying pan. Add the onion and sauté for 2–3 minutes or until translucent. Stir in garlic, ginger and chili and cook for a further 2–3 minutes.
4. Finally, add the shrimp and cauliflower and cook until shrimp they just change color.
5. Stir through tamari, sesame oil and fish sauce. Season to taste and toss through chopped egg, scallions, cilantro and mint. Serve immediately.

EASIEST BUTTER CHICKEN
with Indian spiced pilau

An Indian chef once warned me, "You can't think of calories when cooking butter chicken, as it just won't taste the same." After many, many disasters, I can happily say that this recipe tastes like butter chicken, and there's no ghee, butter or cream yet it still oozes with creaminess and those characteristic warm spices.

INGREDIENTS

2 tablespoons olive oil
1 large brown onion, peeled and diced
4 garlic cloves, peeled and crushed
3 cm (1¼ inch) fresh ginger, grated on a microplane
1 teaspoon garam masala
1 teaspoon ground cumin
½ teaspoon ground coriander
½ teaspoon ground cinnamon
½ teaspoon ground turmeric
½ teaspoon chili powder
1 teaspoon sea salt

750 g (1 lb 8 oz) chicken thigh, skin removed
1 bay leaf
400 g (14 oz) good quality tomato passata (fresh tomato puree)
100 g (3½ oz) roasted, unsalted cashew nuts
200 g (7 oz) gluten free Greek yogurt
2 tablespoons lemon juice
fresh cilantro (coriander) leaves

METHOD

1. Add olive oil to a large saucepan over medium heat. Add the onion, and cook, stirring constantly, until translucent. Add the garlic and ginger, and sauté for a further minute. Turn the heat down to medium and add ground spices and salt (except for bay leaf). Sauté until fragrant, about 2 minutes.
2. Add the chicken to the saucepan and cook for 5 minutes, before adding the bay leaf and passata. Lower the heat and simmer, uncovered, for 20 minutes or until the chicken is cooked through.
3. Meanwhile, place cashews in a mortar and pestle and pound until half the cashews are crushed. Add the crushed cashews, yogurt and lemon juice to the chicken and stir through.
4. Scatter with cilantro and serve immediately with Indian Spiced Pilau (pg 186) or steamed basmati rice.

TERIYAKI SALMON

with fried egg and forbidden rice

This teriyaki salmon is one of my favorite recipes and a weekly staple. I love runny fried eggs—especially when you break the yolk and it mingles through the other ingredients, acting as a gooey, rich sauce.

INGREDIENTS

Black rice
285 g (10 oz) uncooked black rice
750 ml (1½ pint) water
½ teaspoon sea salt

Teriyaki salmon
1 garlic clove, peeled and finely chopped
1 cm (½ inch) fresh ginger, grated in a microplane
3 tablespoons tamari
2 tablespoons mirin (sweet Japanese rice wine) or dry sherry
1 tablespoon pure maple syrup (or sugar)
4 x 180 g (6½ oz) salmon fillets, skin on

1 tablespoon rice bran olive oil
4 free-range eggs, at room temperature
2 tablespoons olive oil
2 (scallions) spring onions, finely sliced
1 tablespoon black (or white) sesame seeds
1 sheet seaweed nori, cut into 1 cm (½ inch) to 2 cm (¾ inch) strips

Sautéed bok choy
4 baby bok choy, quartered or halved lengthways (depending on size)
2 teaspoons rice bran or peanut oil

METHOD

1. To cook the black rice, place the rice in a saucepan with 750ml water and sea salt. Bring to the boil then reduce heat to a simmer and cook, covered for 35 minutes or until rice is cooked. Remove from heat and allow to stand, covered for 5 minutes. The rice should be soft, yet slightly chewy when cooked.
2. Combine all teriyaki ingredients, except the oil in large bowl. Add salmon, toss to coat, cover with plastic wrap and set aside until ready to cook.
3. Meanwhile, place 1 tablespoon olive oil in a frying pan over medium-high. Add 2 eggs and fry until the whites are set but yolks are runny or cooked to your liking (about 3 minutes for soft yolks). Transfer to a plate. Heat remaining 1 tablespoon olive oil and repeat with remaining eggs. Set aside and keep warm.
4. Using the same saucepan, heat 2 teaspoons oil over high heat. Add bok choy and cook for 1 minute, tossing constantly to coat with oil. Add 2 tablespoons water, cover, cook for 1 minute to steam and cook through. Set aside and keep warm.
5. Using the same saucepan, add 1 tablespoon oil and heat to medium-high. Shake off excess marinade and cook salmon, skin side down, until skin is charred. Flip over and cook on the other side. The middle should be pink but the outside caramelized. Depending on the size of your frying pan, you may need to cook the salmon in batches. Just before serving, add the remaining marinade to the pan and cook for 1 minute.
6. To assemble rice bowls, divide rice between the bowls and top with salmon, fried egg and bok choy. Drizzle with remaining sauce from the pan and scatter with scallions, sesame seeds and nori strips.

HAINAN POACHED CHICKEN
with aromatic rice

This version of a famous Singaporean dish is an unassuming mélange of beautiful flavors–from the moist chicken and spicy chili sauce to the aromatic rice. This is comfort food at its best. The chicken needs to sit in the stock for 1½ hours but if you pop the chicken on the stove in the morning, or the night before, this will enhance the flavor and mean it's super simple when you get home.

INGREDIENTS

Poaching liquid
1.5 kg free-range chicken, washed
3 scallions (spring onions), sliced into 3 cm (1¼ inch) batons
1 bunch cilantro (coriander), stalks, roots and leaves, roughly chopped
4 garlic cloves, peeled and lightly crushed
4 cm (1½ inch) piece ginger, sliced
10 black peppercorns

Aromatic rice
1 tablespoon peanut oil
½ brown onion, peeled and finely diced
2 garlic cloves, peeled and finely chopped
120 g (4 oz) jasmine rice
fresh cilantro (coriander)
tamari

Spring onion and chili sauce
4 scallions (spring onions), finely sliced
1 long red chili, finely sliced
1 tablespoon ginger, finely grated
1 teaspoon salt
60 ml (2 fl oz) peanut oil
1 teaspoon sesame oil

METHOD
1. Place the chicken and poaching ingredients in a large saucepan or stockpot. Fill with water to just cover the chicken. Bring to the boil, reduce heat and simmer gently, covered for 15 minutes. Turn off the heat and leave the chicken to cool completely in the stock, about 1½ hours.
2. Meanwhile, to cook the rice. Heat the oil in a small saucepan. Add the onion and garlic and cook until soft. Add the rice, stirring well to coat in the oil. Remove from heat and set aside until the chicken has finished cooling.
3. When the chicken has cooled completely, remove and strain the aromatics from the stock. Add 250 ml (8 fl oz) of the reserved stock to the rice. Bring to the boil, cover and then reduce heat. Simmer for 10–12 minutes or until the liquid has been absorbed. Uncover and fluff the rice with a fork and set aside. Taste and add ½ teaspoon salt, if required.
4. Meanwhile, combine scallions, chili, ginger and salt in a heatproof bowl. Heat oil in a small saucepan until smoking then carefully pour over the scallions. Allow to cool. Stir through sesame oil and set aside.
5. To serve, slice the chicken into thin pieces. Place aromatic rice in the bottom of a bowl, top with chicken and pour over spring onion sauce. Garnish with coriander leaves and serve the stock, together with tamari, as sides.

CAMBODIAN AMOK CURRY

My grandmother, who we fondly call Nanny, first cooked this famous Cambodian steamed fish curry (amok) after a trip to Siem Reap. At 82 years of age, my beautiful Nanny still regularly tries new recipes—most often inspired by a dish she's eaten at a memorable restaurant or on her travels with my grandfather, Hans. This curry has a similar consistency to a soufflé or baked custard. If ling is unavailable, use any firm white fish fillet.

INGREDIENTS

Amok curry paste

6 long dried chilies, seeded and soaked in water for 15 minutes or until soft

2 red Asian shallots (eschalots), peeled and finely diced

6 garlic cloves, peeled and finely chopped

1 teaspoon fresh ginger, grated

2 tablespoons lemongrass, white part only, thinly sliced

1 teaspoon lemon zest, grated using a microplane

3 cilantro (coriander) roots, thinly sliced

½ teaspoon white peppercorns, ground

1 teaspoon shrimp paste

½ teaspoon salt

Curry

150 g (5 oz) Chinese cabbage (wombok), roughly chopped

125 g (4 oz) Thai basil (or regular basil) leaves

60 g (2 oz) amok curry paste (above)

250 ml (8 fl oz) coconut cream

150 g (5 oz) minced fresh ling or finely chopped

300 g (10 oz) fresh ling fillet, or any other firm white fish fillet, skin removed, cut into 1 cm (½ inch) x 2 cm (¾ inch) pieces

2 free-range eggs, lightly beaten

1 tablespoon gluten free fish sauce

2 teaspoons palm sugar

8 kaffir lime leaves, middle vein removed and thinly sliced

1 long red chili, de-seeded and thinly sliced

METHOD

1. For the amok curry paste, place the chili, shallots, garlic, ginger, lemongrass and lemon zest in a mortar and pestle or food processor. Puree to a paste before adding the remaining ingredients. Continue to puree to a paste. Set aside.

2. Bring a large saucepan of water to the boil. Add Chinese cabbage and cook for 2 minutes or until blanched. Remove cabbage, transfer to a colander and run under cold water. Squeeze excess water from cabbage.

3. Fill the bottom of the ramekins with cabbage and then top with a generous amount of Thai basil leaves.

4. In a separate bowl, combine 60 g (2 oz) amok curry paste and coconut cream. Mix until well combined. Add minced fish and stir to combine. Add fish pieces, eggs, fish sauce, palm sugar and kaffir lime leaves and, again, stir to combine. Divide mixture between four 250 ml (8 fl oz) ramekins or bowls.

5. To cook the curry, place a bamboo steamer over a large saucepan filled with water. Bring to the boil and place ramekins inside steamer and cover with the lid. Steam for 10-15 minutes or until just set (the eggs in the mixture give this dish a custard-like consistency). Alternatively, if you don't have a bamboo steamer, preheat oven to 180°C (350°F). Place ramekins in a deep baking dish, fill the base of the dish with at least 2 cm (¾ inch) water. Cook for 10–15 minutes or until just set. Scatter with chili and serve with Steamed Jasmine Rice (pg 185).

CHEEKY CHICKEN SATAY
with cucumber relish

This is my take on a Thai classic (hence the 'cheeky' title). This is a heavily-spiced dish but if you prefer, add some more coconut milk to the marinade and satay sauce as this will temper the heat. Pickles are often served with meals across south-east Asia which is why I've included this cucumber relish—it's very simple but really brings the dish together.

INGREDIENTS

Marinade
2 cloves garlic, peeled and chopped
1 cm (½ inch) fresh ginger, finely grated
1 tablespoon Malaysian curry powder (store bought)
2 teaspoons ground cumin
½ teaspoon ground coriander
½ teaspoon turmeric powder
60 ml (2 fl oz) coconut milk
1 tablespoon rice bran oil (or peanut oil)

Skewers
750 g (1 lb 8 oz) chicken thigh fillets, boneless, skinless, cut into 3 cm (1¼ inch) pieces
2 tablespoons rice bran oil (or peanut oil)
10 long bamboo skewers, soaked in water for 30 minutes

Satay sauce
4 cloves garlic, peeled
2 red Asian shallots (eschalots), peeled and roughly chopped
2 teaspoons Malaysian curry powder (store bought)
½ teaspoon finely grated kaffir lime zest (or lime/lemon zest)
2 kaffir lime leaves, finely chopped
2 tablespoons tamarind puree
2 tablespoons tamari
125 ml (4 fl oz) coconut milk
1 tablespoon gluten free fish sauce
3 tablespoons hulled tahini
2 tablespoons shaved palm sugar

METHOD

1. To make the marinade, combine the garlic, ginger, curry powder, spices, coconut milk and oil in a medium bowl. Add chicken pieces, cover with plastic wrap and marinate for at least 2 hours or preferably overnight.

2. Next, start the satay sauce. In a food processor, blend the garlic and shallots until smooth. Heat a medium saucepan with 1 tablespoon of rice bran oil to medium-high. Add the garlic and shallots from the food processor. Cook until fragrant and lightly golden. Stir through the remaining satay sauce ingredients (curry powder, zest, kaffir lime leaves, tamarind puree, tamari, coconut milk, fish sauce, tahini and palm sugar.) Simmer, uncovered for 10 minutes or until thickened.

3. Thread each piece of chicken lengthwise onto a bamboo skewer. Heat the remaining 1 tablespoon oil in a large frying pan, grill pan or barbecue over medium-high heat. Add skewers, in batches if necessary. Cook, turning occasionally and basting with reserved marinade for 4 minutes or until just cooked through.

4. Place steamed rice in the bottom of the bowl, push chicken pieces off the skewer and top with satay sauce and Cucumber and Chili Relish (pg 151).

SALMON DONBURI

Sushi roll in a bowl

Salmon donburi (literally meaning bowl) is a favorite at our local Japanese restaurant. For me, it ticks all the boxes for a nutritious meal and, to make it at home, all you need is spanking-fresh fish. If you have trouble dicing the salmon, chill it in the freezer for 20 minutes first. You can serve this on steamed brown rice or quinoa too.

INGREDIENTS

450 g (1 lb) sashimi-grade salmon, skin removed and
    pin-boned (or other firm-fleshed sashimi-grade
    fish)
1 avocado, halved, de-stoned and cut into cubes
¼ Spanish onion, peeled and finely diced
3 scallions (spring onions), thinly sliced
2 tablespoons tamari
1 teaspoon sesame oil
1 teaspoon Sriracha sauce
1 cm (½ inch) fresh ginger, finely grated on a
    microplane
pickled ginger (optional)
micro shiso leaves (optional)

Sesame wonton crisps

6 wonton wrappers, each cut diagonally in half to
    form 2 triangles
2 teaspoons olive oil
1 tablespoon black sesame seeds
½ teaspoon sea salt

METHOD

1. Preheat oven to 180°C (350°F).
2. Using a sharp knife, slice salmon into 5 mm (¼ inch) cubes and place in a ceramic (not metal) bowl.
3. Add avocado, Spanish onion, scallions, tamari, sesame oil, Sriracha and ginger. Toss to combine. Cover with plastic wrap and chill in the refrigerator to marinate for 15-30 minutes.
4. Meanwhile, to make the sesame wonton crisps. Line a large oven tray with baking (parchment) paper. Arrange wonton triangles on sheet; brush each with olive oil and sprinkle with sesame seeds and salt. Bake until triangles are golden brown, about 8–9 minutes. Allow to cool.
5. Divide Steamed Sushi Rice (pg 187) among 4 bowls and then top with salmon. Scatter with extra sliced scallions, pickled ginger and micro shiso leaves.

*Sriracha is a Thai chili sauce that can be bought at most supermarkets
and Asian grocers. Shiso, also known as perilla, is a member of the
mint family and is available from select greengrocers.*

SEAFOOD CHOO CHEE CURRY

My gosh, this is the perfect curry with its rich, aromatic paste and creamy, coconut sauce, this is comfort food at its best. Feel free to use any combination of seafood available.

INGREDIENTS

Choo chee paste
10 dried long red chilies
½ teaspoon shrimp paste
1 teaspoon coriander seeds
8 white peppercorns
10 fresh kaffir lime leaves, finely chopped
½ tablespoon zest of kaffir lime (or lime)
2 cilantro (coriander) roots, cleaned, roughly chopped
1 stalk lemon grass, white part only, finely chopped
1 cm (½ inch) fresh ginger, roughly chopped
6 garlic cloves, peeled and roughly chopped
2 red Asian shallots (eschalots), peeled and roughly chopped

Curry
400 ml (14 fl oz) coconut milk, unshaken
100 g (3½ oz) choo chee paste (see above)
375 g (12 oz) green shrimp, peeled and tails on
375 g (12 oz) scallops (roe removed)
150 g (5 oz) snow peas, topped and tailed and outer string removed
2 tablespoons gluten free fish sauce
1 tablespoon palm sugar
12 kaffir lime leaves, middle vein removed and finely sliced
2 long red chilies, de-seeded and cut lengthwise
Steamed Jasmine Rice (pg 185)
2 sprigs fresh cilantro (coriander)

METHOD

1. Soak the dried chilies in hot water for 30 minutes or until softened. Remove from water and roughly chop.
2. Wrap shrimp paste in foil. In a medium frying pan, dry roast coriander seeds, white peppercorns and shrimp paste in foil over medium-high heat for 2–3 minutes or until fragrant. Remove shrimp paste and transfer coriander and peppercorns to a mortar and pestle. Grind to a fine powder.
3. Transfer remaining choo chee paste ingredients to a mortar and pestle or food processor, including the ground spices and shrimp paste to form a smooth paste. If using a mortar and pestle, pound for as long as you can, making sure everything has broken down and combined.
4. To prepare the curry, scoop off the hardened coconut "cream" with a spoon, reserving the remaining milk for later. Add cream to a large wok and cook for 5 minutes or until the cream splits and the oil starts to separate. Stir in the curry paste and simmer, stirring constantly for 5–10 minutes or until fragrant. Stir in the remaining coconut milk, shrimp and snow peas. Cook for 1 minute and then add the scallops. Add the fish sauce, palm sugar and kaffir lime leaves and cook, stirring until the palm sugar dissolves and the scallops and shrimp are just cooked.
5. Divide rice between serving bowls. Pour the curry over the rice and garnish with cilantro. Serve immediately.

Make double the paste and store in the freezer for up to 3 months.

GOAN FISH CURRY

This dish is proof that cooking an Indian curry needn't be time consuming nor require endless ingredients. This fragrant curry is the perfect antidote to cold, dark winter days. The heat from the chili is tempered by a good splash of coconut milk, while the tamarind puree gives the curry a sweet and tangy lift.

INGREDIENTS

2 tablespoons olive oil
1 medium brown onion, finely diced
1 garlic clove, peeled and finely chopped
1 tablespoon ground cumin
1 tablespoon ground coriander
2 teaspoons chili powder
1 teaspoon ground turmeric

½ teaspoon salt
2 x 400 ml (14 fl oz) tinned coconut milk, well shaken
1 tablespoon tamarind puree
2 teaspoons honey (or sugar)
750 g (1 lb 8 oz) ling or any firm white fish, cut into 2 cm (¾ inch) x 3 cm (1¼ inch) pieces
fresh cilantro (coriander)

METHOD

1. Heat oil in a large saucepan to medium-high. Add onion and sauté until lightly golden and translucent. Add the garlic and continue to cook for another minute or until lightly golden.
2. Reduce the heat to low and add the cumin, coriander, chili powder, turmeric and salt. Cook until fragrant for about 1 minute. Pour in the coconut milk, tamarind puree and sugar and stir to combine. Simmer, uncovered for 5–10 minutes or until the curry has thickened. Stir through the ling and cook for 2–3 minutes or until the fish is just cooked through. Scatter with cilantro and serve with Indian Spiced Pilau (pg 186).

NASI GORENG

Nasi goreng, or Indonesian fried rice, is perfect when you're feeling a little run down, or let's be honest, a bit hungover. The shrimp paste and sambal oelek give it a more complex, spicier flavor than a classic Chinese fried rice. Day-old rice works best (it's drier and firmer) but if you do use freshly cooked rice, just be careful not to mash up the grains too much.

INGREDIENTS

2 tablespoons rice bran, peanut or other vegetable oil

½ brown onion, peeled and finely diced

½ teaspoon shrimp paste

1 garlic clove, peeled and finely chopped

1 teaspoon ginger, finely chopped

1 fresh long chili, sliced

500 g (1 lb) leftover/cooked brown rice, cold

1 teaspoon sambal oelek (or chili paste)

1 tablespoon tamari

1 tablespoon kecap manis (Indonesian sweet soy sauce)

4 free-range eggs

1 spring onion, finely sliced

1 tablespoon fried shallots

2 sprigs cilantro (coriander)

1 small cucumber, quartered lengthways and sliced

METHOD

1. Heat half the oil in a wok or large frying pan. Add onion, shrimp paste, garlic, ginger, chili and sambal oelek and cook until lightly golden, about 2–3 minutes.
2. Add rice and toss gently.
3. Stir through soy sauce and kecap manis, and cook until rice is coated.
4. Using a different frying pan, heat remaining oil and fry eggs, cooking only until the whites are just cooked but the yolks are still runny.
5. Fill serving bowl with the nasi goreng and top with fried egg. Scatter with spring onion, fried shallots and cilantro. Serve with cucumber to one side.

*Shrimp paste and fried shallots can be bought at most supermarkets or
Asian grocers.*

BEEF RENDANG
with kaffir lime and coconut rice

Rendang is a boldly-spiced dry Malaysian curry. There's a lot of shrimp paste in this, which acts a bit like anchovy in European cooking—you're hardly aware of it (apart from the initial smell) but you would certainly know if it wasn't there.

INGREDIENTS

Rendang paste

½ teaspoon shrimp paste

4 red Asian shallots (eschalots), peeled and roughly chopped

8 garlic cloves, peeled and chopped

2 cm (¾ inch) ginger, roughly chopped

6 dried red chilies, soaked in hot water for 1 hour, roughly chopped

1 teaspoon ground turmeric

1 teaspoon ground cumin

1 teaspoon ground coriander

Rendang daging

2 tablespoons rice bran oil (or peanut oil)

150 g (5 oz) rendang curry paste (recipe above)

800 g (1 lb 12 oz) chuck steak, cut into 3 cm (1¼ inch) pieces

2 x 400 ml (14 fl oz) coconut milk

2 tablespoons tamarind paste

10 kaffir lime leaves, middle vein removed, thinly sliced

1 cinnamon stick

1 tablespoon palm sugar

50 g (2 oz) desiccated coconut

METHOD

1. Preheat oven to 180°C (350°F).
2. To make the rendang paste, wrap shrimp paste in foil and roast in oven for 10 minutes or until the paste is dry and crumbly. Place the roasted shrimp paste and all remaining paste ingredients in a food processor and process to a smooth paste.
3. Heat a heavy based saucepan to medium-high. Add oil and 150 g (5 oz) curry paste and cook for 2–3 minutes or until fragrant. Add the beef, then stir in the coconut milk, tamarind paste, 6 kaffir lime leaves, cinnamon stick and palm sugar. Reduce heat to a simmer and cook, uncovered, for 1 to 1½ hours or until the beef is tender.
4. Meanwhile, in a frying pan heat desiccated coconut and toast until lightly golden, stirring constantly so the coconut doesn't burn. Once beef is tender, stir toasted coconut through rendang.
5. Garnish with remaining 4 kaffir lime leaves and serve with Steamed Coconut and Kaffir Lime Rice (pg 184).

SEA FARE

My brother Hugh loved fishing. He would spend countless hours down on the jetty or at the beach just fishing. It always astounded me that Hugh, who loved technology so much, working as a mechanical engineer and as someone who bought every electronic gadget ever invented, could enjoy something as simple as fishing so much. Perhaps what shocked me more than that was the fact that regardless of whether he caught something, he always came home in good spirits.

I may not be a keen "fisherlady" but one of my favorite activities is to visit the fish markets. Forget clothes shopping, I walk around, chatting to all the fish mongers, asking what's best that day, perhaps sampling a few oysters, a slice of sashimi and, most importantly, coming home with a bagful of the freshest seafood I can find to cook that night. There are few dishes that give me greater pleasure than Pan Fried Barramundi with Sweet Potato Wedges and Tartare Sauce (pg 77), or Baked Side of Salmon with Tahini Yogurt and Herb Crust (pg 72).

Nothing says summer like seafood, grilled on the barbecue. All you need is fresh seafood and the effort-to-reward ratio is high. These tried and tested seafood dishes have come out of my kitchen many, many times. Some are simple, some require a bit of time to prepare, but none will fail you.

STEAMED MUSSELS

with coconut and lemongrass broth

I love to serve these mussels in a big pot in the middle of the table—after a few drinks, everyone is helping themselves, slurping from the shells and splashing it all over their clothes. It's a happy, slapdash affair that never fails to get a laugh (and a few requests for the recipe).

INGREDIENTS

1 long red chili, de-seeded, finely chopped
3 garlic cloves, peeled and finely chopped
½ Spanish onion, peeled and finely diced
½ bunch flat-leaf parsley, roughly chopped
½ bunch cilantro (coriander), roughly chopped
1 lemongrass stalk (white part only), thinly sliced

1 kg (2 lb) black mussels, scrubbed and de-bearded
2 tablespoons extra virgin olive oil
125 ml (4 fl oz) dry white wine
150 ml (5 fl oz) coconut milk
fresh cilantro (coriander) leaves

METHOD

1. In a large bowl, combine chili, garlic, Spanish onion, parsley, cilantro and lemongrass. Add the mussels and toss to combine.
2. Heat olive oil in a large saucepan until it begins to smoke. Add mussels and cook for 10 seconds, then stir through white wine, followed by the coconut milk.
3. Cover with a tight-fitting lid and cook, shaking pan continuously, over high heat for 3–4 minutes or until mussels have opened.
4. Divide Steamed Jasmine Rice (pg 185) between four bowls. Top with mussels and coconut milk sauce, scatter with cilantro and serve immediately.

VIETNAMESE VERMICELLI BUN

with lemongrass prawn cakes and nuoc cham

This Vietnamese vermicelli bun (noodle salad) is a beautiful contrast of flavors and textures—from the lemongrass-spiked prawn cakes to the fragrant, herbaceous salad with toasted peanuts and fried shallots. The classic Vietnamese sauce, nuoc cham, makes this dish, however it's dangerously hot, so de-seed the chilies if you prefer, or use a long red chili instead, which is milder.

INGREDIENTS

Prawn cakes

2 garlic cloves, peeled and finely chopped
1 cm (½ inch) ginger, grated on a microplane
1 stalk lemongrass, white part only, finely chopped
½ small brown onion, peeled and finely diced
1 teaspoon sambal oelek (or chili paste)
1 teaspoon fish sauce
½ bunch cilantro (coriander), roughly chopped
2 cilantro (coriander) roots, cleaned and finely
   chopped
1 free-range egg white
500 g (1 lb) green shrimp (prawns), peeled, deveined
   and roughly chopped
rice bran oil spray

Salad

250 g (9 oz) dried rice noodle vermicelli
1 carrot, peeled
2 Lebanese cucumbers, thinly sliced lengthways 4
   scallions (spring onions), thinly sliced
½ bunch mint, roughly chopped
½ bunch cilantro (coriander), roughly chopped
2 tablespoons roasted peanuts, roughly chopped
1 tablespoon fried shallots (optional)

Nuoc cham

3 tablespoons white vinegar
1 tablespoon superfine (castor) sugar
3 tablespoons lime juice
2 tablespoons fish sauce
1 red birds eye chili, finely chopped
1 garlic clove, peeled and crushed

METHOD

1. Preheat oven to 180°C (350°F).
2. Using a blender or food processor, combine all prawn cake ingredients (including the shrimp) and blend to a paste. Prepare a tray lined with baking (parchment) paper and spray with rice bran oil. Using two tablespoons, create walnut-sized quenelles or balls with the prawn mixture and place on the tray. Spray prawn cakes with oil and roast in oven for 15 minutes, turning every 5 minutes or until lightly golden. (You can shallow fry the prawn cakes in a heavy-based saucepan.)
3. Cook the noodles by placing rice vermicelli in a medium bowl and covering completely with boiling water. Cover with plastic wrap and leave for 15–20 minutes or until softened. Drain and rinse with cold water.
4. Meanwhile, prepare the salad. Slice peeled carrot, lengthways, into long strips or ribbons. In a large bowl, combine carrot, cucumber ribbons and the herbs. Toss to combine. To make the nuoc cham, combine ingredients in a bowl and season.
5. To assemble your bun, divide the vermicelli noodles between bowls. Top with salad and prawn cakes. Drizzle each bowl generously with nuoc cham and scatter with roasted peanuts and fried shallots.

SHRIMP LAKSA

There's nothing quite like sipping and slurping a big bowl of spicy laksa, where the noodles splash over your clothes, no matter how delicately you attempt to eat it and the spiciness leaves a layer of sweat on your brow. You don't need to make the laksa from scratch—a good quality laksa paste will do the trick.

INGREDIENTS

Laksa paste*
2 dried chilies, soaked for 30 minutes in boiling water, roughly chopped
1 teaspoon coriander seeds
2 teaspoons shrimp paste, roasted in oven (see below)
2 red Asian shallots (eschalots), peeled and diced
6 garlic cloves
1 teaspoon lime zest
1 stalk lemongrass, white part only, finely chopped
1 teaspoon galangal
4 small red chilies, finely chopped
25 g macadamia nuts, roughly chopped
1 tablespoon tamarind puree
1 teaspoon turmeric powder

* can use a good store-purchased laksa paste

Laksa
250 g (9 oz) rice vermicelli noodles, soaked in boiling water until *al dente*, and drained
750 ml (1½ pint) coconut cream, chilled and unshaken
3 tablespoons laksa paste
125 ml (4 fl oz) good quality stock, chicken, vegetable or fish
1 tablespoon gluten free fish sauce
1 tablespoon tamari
1 teaspoon palm sugar
750 g (1 lb 8 oz) green shrimp (prawns), deveined and peeled with tail intact
150 g (5 oz) fried tofu puffs, halved
1 small cucumber, sliced
½ bunch mint leaves
100 g (3½ oz) bean sprouts
1 lime, cut into quarters

METHOD

1. If you're making your paste from scratch, preheat oven to 180°C (350°F). (Otherwise, skip to the next step). Wrap shrimp paste in foil and roast in oven for 10 minutes or until dry and crumbly. In a medium saucepan, dry roast coriander seeds and then transfer to a mortar and pestle and pound to a ground spice. Combine all remaining ingredients in a food processor (or mortar and pestle) and blend until smooth.
2. To cook the vermicelli, place the noodles in a medium bowl and cover completely with boiling water. Cover with plastic wrap and leave for 15–20 minutes or until softened. Drain noodles and rinse with cold water.
3. In a medium saucepan, heat oil to medium. Add laksa paste and a tablespoon of the thick top layer of coconut cream. Cook for a few minutes or until aromatic. Add the remaining coconut cream, stock, fish sauce, tamari and palm sugar. Stir through the shrimp and tofu puffs and simmer for 2–3 minutes. Check seasoning and divide noodles between bowls. Pour over laksa and top with cucumber, mint, bean sprouts and a lime wedge, on the side.

HOMEMADE TORTILLA BOWL
with shrimp, guacamole and pico de gallo

Fill your crunchy tortilla bowl with seared spiced shrimp, creamy guacamole and sweet-and-sour 'slaw for a healthy and satisfying meal. Pico de gallo, also called salsa fresca, is a fresh, uncooked salad made with chopped tomato, cilantro (coriander), lemon juice and chili. For a Tex Mex twist, add shredded cheese and a dollop of sour cream.

INGREDIENTS

4 burrito-size tortillas
olive oil cooking spray
1 tablespoon olive oil
1 lime, juiced
1 teaspoon ground cumin
1 teaspoon ground coriander
½ teaspoon ground chili
500 g (1 lb) green shrimp (prawns), peeled, deveined
Red Cabbage and Nashi Pear Slaw (pg 113), optional

Pico de gallo

10 cherry tomatoes, quartered
2 tablespoons fresh cilantro (coriander), roughly
    chopped

1 tablespoon lime juice
1 small red chili, finely chopped
1 tablespoon olive oil

Guacamole

1 ripe avocado
1 lime, juiced
1 tablespoon extra virgin olive oil
1 teaspoon ground cumin
1 garlic clove, peeled and finely chopped
½ bunch cilantro (coriander), roughly chopped

METHOD

1. Preheat oven to 180°C (350°F).
2. Spray the inside of four oven-safe bowls with cooking oil. Gently press one tortilla inside each of the bowls. Transfer to a baking tray and cook for 15 minutes or until evenly browned. Allow tortillas to cool in the bowls for 5 minutes before transferring to a wire rack.
3. In a bowl, combine the oil, lime juice, cumin, cilantro and chili. Add shrimp and toss to coat. Set aside.
4. To make pico de gallo, combine all ingredients in a small bowl. Season and set aside. The longer this can marinate, the better.
5. To make guacamole, cut the avocadoes in half, remove the pit, score both ways and then scoop out the flesh with a spoon and place in a large bowl. Use the back of a fork to mash until almost smooth. Add the lime juice, olive oil, cumin, garlic and cilantro and mix well. Taste and season with salt and pepper.
6. Heat a chargrill pan to high. Add shrimp, in batches if necessary, and cook for 2 minutes on each side or until shrimp until it turns pink.
7. If using the slaw, drain off excess salad dressing and place in the bottom of the crisp tortilla bowl. Top with guacamole, shrimp and scatter with pico de gallo.

SQUID INK LINGUINE

Making pasta from scratch is one of those processes that once you've done it, you'll think "Why haven't I been doing this all my life?" This pasta is made using squid ink to give it that beautiful black color however it doesn't have a strong flavor. I prefer to use "00" flour for pasta as it has a higher gluten content than plain flour and makes a more elastic dough. If unavailable, substitute plain flour.

INGREDIENTS

Squid ink pasta dough*
2 tablespoons squid ink
1 tablespoon olive oil
300 g (10 oz) fine 00 (extra fine) flour
3 free-range eggs
3 teaspoons sea salt
* can replace with store-bought linguine

Squid ink linguine
800 g (1 lb 12 oz) baby squid

2 tablespoons olive oil
6 garlic cloves, peeled and finely chopped
1 long red chili, deseeded and chopped
2 tablespoons lemon juice
50 ml white wine
sea salt and freshly ground pepper
2 tablespoons extra virgin olive oil
3 sprigs flat-leaf parsley, roughly chopped
1 lemon, cut into wedges

METHOD

1. Start by making the dough. In a small bowl, combine squid ink and olive oil. Using a food processor, add flour, eggs and salt and process until just combined, about 10 seconds. Then add combined oil and squid ink mixture and process until it forms a dough. Try not to overwork the dough—you just want the ingredients to combine. Remove and shape dough into 4 discs, wrap each in plastic wrap and refrigerate for 30 minutes.

2. Meanwhile, prepare squid. Cut off tentacles and set aside. Cut squid tubes open, clean innards and score the inside flesh in a criss-cross pattern. Make sure you don't cut all the way through. Cut squid into 3 cm (1¼ inch) x 5 cm (2 inch) pieces.

3. Working in batches, roll your pasta through a pasta-making machine, starting at the thickest setting and working through to the smallest setting. Repeat with each batch of pasta. Keep dough that you're not using sealed in plastic wrap or underneath a damp towel. Work as quickly as possible with the dough because the pasta will dry out quickly.

4. Cut pasta into 5 mm (¼ inch)-wide strips in the pasta machine (to make linguine) and hang in a single layer over a damp tea towel-lined hanger (you can also use the back of a chair).

5. To cook pasta, bring a large pot of salted water to the boil. Add pasta, in batches and cook for 2–3 minutes or until *al dente* (the pasta should still have a slight bite). Drain, set aside and repeat until all the pasta is cooked. Reserve cooking water.

6. Place olive oil in a large frying pan and heat to medium. Add garlic and chili. Cook for 3 minutes or until lightly golden. Increase heat to high and add squid pieces. Cook, tossing occasionally for 3 minutes or until just cooked and still tender.

7. Add lemon juice, white wine and about 1–2 tablespoons of reserved water from pasta. Toss through the cooked pasta and heat through. Taste and season with salt and pepper (it may be salty enough with the squid). If the pasta looks a little dry, add more of the reserved cooking water to loosen it slightly.

8. Drizzle with extra virgin olive oil and scatter with chopped parsley. Serve with a lemon wedge on the side.

BAKED SIDE OF SALMON

with tahini yogurt and herb crust

This Turkish-inspired dish makes an impressive meal for any occasion, especially when served as a whole side in the middle of the table, with bowls of Crunchy Cauliflower, Quinoa and Almond Salad. Don't be intimidted by the amount of sumac—the sweet yet tangy flavor it imparts is a key ingredient in the herb crust.

INGREDIENTS

1 kg (2 lb) side of salmon (or ocean trout), pin-boned
  and skin left on
2 tablespoons extra virgin olive oil
sea salt

3 tablespoons walnuts, finely chopped
2 tablespoons sumac*
½ teaspoon sea salt
1 tablespoon olive oil

Herb crust

½ Spanish onion, peeled and finely diced
1 bunch cilantro (coriander), roughly chopped
1 bunch flat-leaf parsley, roughly chopped
1 bunch mint, roughly chopped
2 long red chilies, de-seeded and finely chopped
3 tablespoons blanched almonds, finely chopped

Tahini dressing

100 g (3½ oz) gluten free Greek yogurt
2 tablespoons tahini
2 tablespoons lemon juice
1 teaspoon ground cumin
1 garlic clove, peeled and crushed

METHOD

1. Preheat oven to 180°C (350°F).
2. Rub salmon with olive oil and season with salt. Place salmon, skin side down, on a baking tray large enough to fit the salmon. Cook for 15–20 minutes or until the fish is just cooked but still a little pink in the middle. Remove and allow to cool.
3. Meanwhile, to prepare the herb crust, place all the ingredients in a food processor. Blitz in 10-second bursts until all ingredients are just combined (but not completely processed—you still want texture). Taste and season with salt and pepper, as required.
4. To make the tahini dressing, place all the ingredients in a medium bowl. Whisk to form a thick paste.
5. Once the salmon is at room temperature, spread tahini dressing on top, then evenly scatter with the herb crust to completely coat the fish. Serve with Crunchy Cauliflower, Quinoa and Almond Salad (pg 140).

Sumac is used in a lot of Middle Eastern cooking and can be bought at any good grocer or delicatessen.

SHRIMP AND XO SAUCE

with soba noodles

XO is a rich, complex Chinese sauce that is delicious with seafood and particularly shrimp. Served with soba noodles (Japanese buckwheat noodles), which are a great source of amino acids and fiber, this is a great weeknight dish, especially as you can do the XO sauce ahead of time.

INGREDIENTS

XO sauce

50 g (2 oz) dried shrimp, soaked in hot water for 30 minutes
8 garlic cloves, peeled and roughly chopped
2 tablespoon ginger, finely chopped
8 long red chilies, seeds left in, roughly chopped
100 g (3½ oz) red shallots, peeled and finely diced
100 ml (3½ oz) rice bran oil or any neutral oil with a high smoking point
3 teaspoons light palm sugar
90 ml (3 fl oz) Shaoxing wine
1 teaspoon sesame oil
120 ml (4 fl oz) tamari

Stir fry

1 tablespoon rice bran oil (or peanut oil)
600 g (1 lb 5 oz) raw green shrimp (prawns), peeled (tails intact) and deveined
2 free-range egg whites, lightly beaten
90 ml (3 fl oz) prawn or chicken stock
250 g (9 oz) soba noodles
80 g (3 oz) XO sauce
1 lime, cut into wedges
fresh micro cilantro (coriander) leaves

METHOD

1. For the XO sauce, drain the dried shrimp and roughly chop. Place dried shrimp in a food processor with garlic, ginger, chili and shallots and process until combined.
2. Add 100 ml (3½ oz) rice bran oil to a wok and heat to medium. Add the garlic mixture from the food processor. Cook for 5–6 minutes, then add the palm sugar. Cook for a few minutes then de-glaze the wok with Shaoxing wine. Stir through the sesame oil and tamari sauce, reduce heat to low and simmer uncovered for 15 minutes.
3. Meanwhile, cook the soba noodles. Bring a large pot of salted water to boil. Add the soba noodles and cook until tender, but still *al dente*, about 5–8 minutes (check with the packet instructions). Drain, rinse well under cold water and set aside. Once XO sauce is cooked, reserve 80 g to stir fry. Store remaining XO sauce in a sterilized jar. It will keep in the refrigerator or freezer for up to 6 months.
4. To cook the shrimp, heat 1 tablespoon oil in the same wok over high heat. Add half the shrimp and cook, tossing regularly until they turn opaque, about 1 minute. Set aside and repeat with remaining shrimp. Return all the shrimp to the wok, add reserved XO sauce and toss to coat. Stir through beaten egg whites and swirl until the egg sets against the wok. Pour in stock and quickly stir through.
5. Divide soba noodles between bowls and top with XO shrimp. Scatter with cilantro and serve with a wedge of lime and a dollop of XO sauce.

SHRIMP AND FETTA SAGANAKI

Saganaki, named after the frying pan in which the dish is prepared, is a Greek favorite. I suggest serving this dish straight from the pan—which not only allows you to scoop up all the delicious tomato sauce—but also saves time in the washing up department.

INGREDIENTS

60 ml (2 fl oz) olive oil
1 Spanish onion, peeled and finely diced
½ red bell pepper (capsicum), chopped
3 garlic cloves, peeled and finely chopped
1 long red chili, deseeded and finely chopped
125 ml (4 fl oz) dry white wine
1 tablespoon tomato paste

400 g (14 oz) tinned diced tomatoes
600 g (1 lb 5 oz) raw green shrimp (prawns), peeled
   and de-veined, tails intact
½ bunch flat-leaf parsley, roughly chopped
150 g (5 oz) fetta, cubed
sea salt and freshly ground pepper
crusty bread (optional)

METHOD

1. Preheat grill oven.
2. Heat the olive oil in a deep-sided frying pan to medium-high. Add the onion and bell pepper and sauté for 5 minutes, or until soft and translucent. Add the garlic and chili and cook for 1 minute. Deglaze the pan with white wine and then add tomato paste and tinned tomatoes. Stir to combine and then add shrimp and parsley. Cook for 2 minutes or until shrimp starts to become pink. Scatter with fetta, then transfer to the oven and place under grill for 5–10 minutes or until the fetta turns lightly golden.
3. Scatter with flat-leaf parsley and serve immediately, with crusty bread if desired.

PAN FRIED BARRAMUNDI
with sweet potato wedges and gherkin tartare

I could eat this dish every single night. Duck fat is the most ridiculously delicious stuff for roasting these sweet potato wedges (keep the skin on the sweet potato as it's full of antioxidants).This recipe is grain-free, sugar-free and gluten free so it's a great one to have up your sleeve for any guests with allergies or dietary requirements.

INGREDIENTS

4 x 150 g (5 oz) barramundi fillets, skin on, pin-boned
   and scales removed
3 tablespoons extra virgin olive oil
sea salt and freshly ground black pepper

Gherkin tartare

3 tablespoons Whole Egg Mayonnaise (pg 181)
3 gherkins, finely chopped

2 tablespoons fresh flat-leaf parsley, finely chopped
1 tablespoon lemon juice
1 teaspoon capers, drained and finely chopped

Sweet potato wedges

500 g (1 lb) sweet potato
3 tablespoons duck fat (or olive oil)
sea salt and pepper

METHOD

1. Preheat oven to 200ºC (400ºF).
2. Cut sweet potatoes into even sized wedges and place in a large bowl. Toss with melted duck fat and season generously with salt and pepper. Place sweet potatoes on a lined baking tray, in a single layer and roast in the oven for 30–40 minutes or until golden and crunchy.
3. Meanwhile, to make tartare sauce, place all ingredients in a small bowl and mix to combine. I like my tartare quite chunky so I don't cut up the gherkins or parsley too much. Taste and add a little more lemon juice, if you prefer.
4. Once the sweet potatoes are almost cooked. Season barramundi skin generously with salt and pepper. Heat olive oil in a large frying pan to medium-high. Add barramundi, skin-side down first, and cook for 3–4 minutes or until the skin is crispy. Flip over and cook for a further 2 minutes.
5. Stack the sweet potato wedges in the bottom of your bowl, top with fish and tartare sauce.

CRUNCHY COCONUT SHRIMP
with ginger and chili syrup and mango and avocado salsa

Mangoes, shrimp and coconut are a marriage made in heaven and hit the spot on a hot summer night. Rather than deep frying the shrimp in batter, the shredded coconut crisps up in the pan. Be careful, once the shrimp hits the pan, it'll cook through quickly.

INGREDIENTS

Ginger and chili syrup
4 tablespoons sugar
4 tablespoons water
2 cm (¾ inch) fresh ginger, peeled and julienned
1 long red chili, finely chopped

Coconut shrimp
600 g (1 lb 5 oz) raw green shrimp (prawns), deveined, peeled and tails intact
1 teaspoon sea salt flakes
½ teaspoon Sichuan peppercorns, ground in a mortar and pestle
¼ teaspoon freshly ground black pepper
¼ teaspoon chili flakes
80 g (3 oz) shredded coconut (or desiccated)

2 egg whites, lightly beaten
4 tablespoons olive oil

Salsa
½ mango, diced
1 large red chili, deseeded and thinly sliced
2 scallions (spring onions), sliced
½ avocado, diced
1 small Lebanese cucumber, diced
2 tablespoons tamarind puree
2 tablespoons lime juice (or lemon)
1 tablespoon gluten free fish sauce
½ bunch cilantro (coriander) leaves
½ bunch mint leaves

METHOD

1. To make the ginger and chili syrup, add the sugar and water in a small saucepan over high heat. Cook for a few minutes stirring until the sugar dissolves. Add the ginger and chili. Bring to boil and cook for 5–8 minutes or until slightly thickened. Set aside and keep warm.
2. Meanwhile, combine salt, Sichuan peppercorns, pepper, chili flakes and coconut in a small bowl. Lightly beat egg whites in a separate bowl and then dip each prawn in egg white, followed by the coconut and spice mixture. Toss to coat, then shake off any excess egg white. Set aside.
3. To make salad, combine all ingredients in a large bowl and gently toss to combine.
4. To cook the shrimp, heat olive oil in a frying pan or wok to medium-high. Add shrimp in batches and cook, turning regularly until lightly golden. Remove using a slotted spoon. Drain on absorbent paper and keep warm. Continue with remaining shrimp. Divide salad between bowls, top with crunchy shrimp and either drizzle with ginger and chili syrup or serve as a side.

Sichuan peppercorns can be bought from most gourmet grocers and Asian supermarkets.

BLACKENED SALMON

with grilled peach and mozzarella salad

We bring the powers of the grill to the salad bowl in this dish—smoky, Cajun-spiced salmon, charred ripe peaches, chewy mozzarella and bitter rocket (arugula). Nectarines, and most stone fruits, can be used in place of the peaches but a ripe pear or even a fig would also work well.

INGREDIENTS

Blackened salmon
4 x 160 g (5½ oz) salmon fillets, pin-boned, skin on
3 tablespoons olive oil
1 tablespoon paprika
1 tablespoon dried thyme
2 teaspoons cayenne pepper
2 teaspoons dried oregano
1 teaspoon garlic powder (optional)
½ teaspoon sea salt
½ teaspoon freshly ground black pepper

Dressing
3 tablespoons red wine vinegar
3 tablespoons extra virgin olive oil
2 teaspoons honey
sea salt and freshly ground black pepper

Salad
2 large yellow peaches (substitute any variety)
2 ripe avocados
150 g (5 oz) baby rocket (arugula) leaves
125 g (4 oz) grape tomatoes, halved lengthways
100 g (3½ oz) fresh mozzarella (or fetta substitute),
    torn into bite size pieces

METHOD

1. Coat the salmon with 1 tablespoon olive oil.
2. In a small bowl, combine the paprika, thyme, cayenne, oregano, garlic powder (if using), salt and pepper and mix to combine. Place the spices on a plate and coat the portions of salmon pieces, on all sides except the skin. Set aside while you prepare the salad.
3. To make the salad dressing, whisk to combine the vinegar, olive oil and honey in a small bowl. Season, to taste, with salt and pepper.
4. Halve the peaches and remove the stones, then cut into even wedges. Repeat with the avocado.
5. Brush a grill pan with a little olive oil and heat to medium-high. Place peach wedges on the pan and grill for 2–3 minutes or until charred lines appear. Flip onto the other side and cook for a further 2–3 minutes. Allow to cool slightly.
6. Add remaining 2 tablespoons oil in a large frying pan and heat to medium. Once oil is hot, add the salmon, skin side down. Cook for 5–6 minutes or until the skin is crispy. Use a spatula to turn the salmon over and cook for 2–3 minutes or until it turns a charred, blackened color. Set aside, skin side up, and rest for a few minutes.
7. In a large bowl, combine the grilled peach wedges, avocado, baby rocket, cherry tomatoes and mozzarella. Drizzle with dressing and divide between the bowls.
8. Top with the blackened salmon and serve immediately.

SUPER BOWLS

On busy days, dinner is often the only meal that allows us to sit down with friends and family at the table and eat together. We live in such an increasingly disconnected world that I find myself craving these times when I can slow down and appreciate good food, but most importantly, to spend time with the people I love.

Super bowls are my hearty, meat-based bowls. In this chapter, you'll find dishes that can be thrown together when you're in a hurry and some that you need to spend more time on such as the Braised Beef Cheeks in Aromatic Spices (pg 89) or Slow Roasted Lamb Shoulder with Harissa-spiced Crushed Carrots (pg 87). Many of these dishes are great for feeding a crowd, such as the Sweet Spiced Duck Marylands with Chili and Plums (pg 100), Maple Bourbon Pork Belly Bites (pg 92) and Filipino Chicken Adobo (pg 90). You can easily double or even triple these recipes and they can all be done ahead of time.

SPICED YOGURT SPATCHCOCK
with carrot, almond and cilantro salad

This is one recipe loved by the whole Lisle family. I vividly remember when the house was filled with the sweet aroma of Mum cooking this dish. Butterflying the spatchcock (a technique also called spatchcocking—confusing, I know) is used to preserve the bird's moisture and it also speeds up the cooking time.

INGREDIENTS

4 x 500 g (1 lb) free-range spatchcock (or chicken)
2 tablespoons extra virgin olive oil
2 teaspoons cumin seeds
1 teaspoon coriander seeds
1 teaspoon ground turmeric
½ teaspoon cardamom powder (optional)
½ teaspoon dried chili flakes
2 garlic cloves, peeled and roughly chopped
1 cm (½ inch) fresh ginger, finely grated

Honey yogurt sauce
200 g (7 oz) gluten free natural yogurt
1 teaspoon honey, heated

Carrot, almond and cilantro salad
75 g (3 oz) flaked almonds
4 carrots, peeled, cut into julienne on a mandoline or
    into ribbons using a spiralizer (you can also just
    grate the carrots)
100 g (3½ oz) sultanas, soaked in warm water for 5
    minutes, drained
½ bunch cilantro (coriander), roughly chopped
sea salt and freshly cracked pepper
2 tablespoon extra virgin olive oil
1 tablespoon white wine vinegar

METHOD

1. Preheat oven to 200°C (400°F).
2. To butterfly spatchcock, use kitchen scissors to cut down either side of the backbone then remove (reserve the backbones for stock). Remove offal and gristle from cavity and discard. On a chopping board, firmly press down on the breastbone to flatten. Carefully separate the skin from the breast, thigh and drumstick meat to create a pocket.
3. In a medium frying pan, dry roast cumin and coriander seeds for 2–3 minutes or until fragrant. Allow spices to cool, and then grind in a mortar and pestle. Add turmeric, cardamom, chili flakes, garlic and ginger and pound to a paste.
4. Combine the yogurt and honey in a bowl. Reserve half this yogurt for serving. Add the remaining half to the spice mix and stir to combine. Push spiced yogurt under the skin of the spatchcock where you created a pocket (both breasts and legs making sure you don't rip the skin). Rub olive oil over the skin to coat and generously season with salt and pepper. Leave to marinate for at least 30 minutes or up to 2 hours in the refrigerator.
5. Transfer to a baking tray large enough to fit the butterflied spatchcocks, in a single layer. Roast for 15–18 minutes or until just cooked. You may need to turn up the oven to 220°C (425°F) for the last 5 minutes to get the skin crispy but be careful not to overcook the spatchcock. Take the spatchcock out and rest in a warm place for 5 minutes.
6. Meanwhile, prepare the salad. Scatter almonds on an oven tray and roast, shaking occasionally, until lightly golden (3–5 minutes). Allow to cool. Combine remaining salad ingredients in a bowl and toss to combine.
7. Divide salad between bowls. Halve spatchcock and serve with pan juices spooned over and scatter with cilantro to serve.

SICHUAN PEPPER BEEF
with cashews and egg noodles

This bold, Chinese-inspired stir-fry uses Sichuan peppercorns, which aren't pungent like black pepper, they're more aromatic and tangy which create a numbing sensation in the mouth. Make sure all your vegetables are prepped and the sauce is ready, as the stir fry is ready within a matter of minutes

INGREDIENTS

500 g (1 lb) fresh thin egg noodles (substitute with dried egg noodles cooked to packet instructions)

3 tablespoons rice bran oil (or any neutral oil)

2 x 300 g (10 oz) scotch fillet steaks, trimmed of fat, thinly sliced

Sichuan sauce

1 brown onion, peeled and sliced lengthways

3 garlic cloves, peeled and finely chopped

2 cm (¾ inch) fresh ginger, finely grated

4 dried red chilies, deseeded and roughly chopped

1 tablespoon Sichuan peppercorns, coarsely ground

4 tablespoons tamari

4 tablespoons Shaoxing rice wine

1 teaspoon sesame oil

125 ml (4 fl oz) chicken stock, salt reduced

1 tablespoon sugar

200 g (7 oz) broccoli, cut into small florets

4 scallions (spring onions), cut into 3 cm (1¼ inch) lengths

75 g (3 oz) dry roasted cashew nuts, unsalted

METHOD

1. Bring a saucepan of salted water to the boil to cook the noodles until *al dente*, about 1 minute. Drain well, set aside and keep warm.
2. Add 2 tablespoons of the oil to a wok or large frying pan and heat to high. Add the beef, in batches, and cook until just seared. Remove from wok and set aside.
3. Add the remaining 1 tablespoon oil, onion, garlic, ginger, chilies and ground peppercorns and stir-fry for about 1 minute, or until fragrant. Add tamari, Shaoxing, sesame oil, stock, sugar and broccoli. Cook until broccoli is just tender. Return beef to the wok together with scallions and cashew nuts. Stir-fry to coat (above 1 minute) and season to taste.
4. Add egg noodles to bowls. Top with Sichuan beef and serve immediately.

Fresh egg noodles, Shaoxing wine and Sichuan peppercorns can be bought from most gourmet grocers and Asian supermarkets.

SLOW ROASTED LAMB SHOULDER
with harissa-spiked crushed carrots

Growing up on a sheep farm, I was lucky to enjoy lamb for dinner most nights and one of my favorite cuts has always been lamb shoulder—simply cooked, without too many trimmings, where the end result does the meat proud. After 8 hours in the oven, the lamb emerges succulent, fragrant and falling-off-the-bone tender.

INGREDIENTS
Lamb shoulder
1.2 kg (2 lb 10 oz) lamb shoulder
2 tablespoon black peppercorns
10 garlic cloves
1 tablespoon salt
2 brown onions, skin on and sliced into rounds
60 ml (2 fl oz) olive oil
3 sprigs rosemary
3 sprigs thyme

Harissa-spiked crushed carrots
2 tablespoons extra virgin olive oil

1 tablespoon unsalted butter
1 kg (2 lb) carrots, peeled and cut into 1 cm (½ inch)
   slices
1 garlic clove, peeled and finely chopped
300 ml (10 fl oz) chicken stock
1 teaspoon harissa paste
1 teaspoon honey
125 g (4 oz) gluten free Greek yogurt
1 tablespoon lemon juice
sea salt and freshly ground pepper
2 sprigs cilantro (coriander)

METHOD
1. Preheat oven to 150°C (300°F).
2. Using a sharp knife, score the lamb shoulder all over in a criss-cross pattern. Using a mortar and pestle, grind peppercorns, garlic and salt to a paste. Add a good splash of oil and mix to form a loose paste. Smear the marinade over the meat and rub into the skin.
3. Place the onion in the base of a large, heavy ovenproof dish. Place lamb on top of onions. Pour 250 ml (8 fl oz) water into the base of the dish and scatter lamb with rosemary and thyme sprigs. Cover entire dish tightly with two sheets of foil. Roast for 8 hours or until meat pulls away from the bone.
4. Meanwhile, prepare the harissa carrots. Heat oil and butter in a large frying pan to medium-high. Add carrots and garlic. Stir often until they start to caramelize slightly, about 5 minutes. Add stock, reduce heat to medium-low and cover. Cook for a further 30 minutes or until the carrots are completely soft. Transfer softened carrots to a bowl and crush the carrots to form a coarse mash using the back of a fork. Alternatively, use a food processor however don't over blend. Stir through the harissa paste, honey, yogurt, lemon juice, salt and pepper.
5. Pull lamb off the bone into pieces, serve with crushed carrots and scatter with cilantro.

MIDDLE EASTERN KOFTA
with rich tomato sauce

Meatballs are about as down-to-earth as a dish can get and these Middle Eastern spiced ones are supernaturally good: hearty, saucy and spiked with pine nuts. I've used a combination of beef and pork mince, which give a lovely texture and taste however you can substitute with lamb mince.

INGREDIENTS

Kofta
400 g (14 oz) beef mince
400 g (14 oz) pork mince
1 small brown onion, diced
2 garlic cloves, peeled and finely chopped
2 free-range eggs, lightly beaten
50 g (2 oz) pine nuts
½ bunch flat-leaf parsley, roughly chopped
2 teaspoons ground cinnamon
2 teaspoons ground allspice
2 teaspoons ground cumin
2 teaspoons ground black pepper
2 teaspoons salt
2 tablespoons olive oil
2 tablespoons unsalted butter

Rich tomato sauce
1 tablespoon olive oil
2 garlic cloves, peeled and finely chopped
1 small brown onion, peeled and finely diced
60 ml (2 fl oz) red wine
2 tablespoons tomato paste
2 x 400 g (14 oz) tinned diced tomato

Cous Cous
300 g (10 oz) cous cous
2 tablespoons butter
sea salt and freshly ground pepper

Garnish
Greek yogurt
fresh cilantro (coriander)

METHOD

1. Place all the kofta ingredients, except olive oil and butter, in a large bowl and use your hands to combine, working the mixture until it forms a smooth texture. Shape into balls (about 2 tablespoons for each ball) and set aside.
2. To make the tomato sauce, place olive oil in a saucepan and heat to medium. Add garlic and onion and sauté until softened, about 5 minutes. Add wine and cook until the liquid reduces a little, about 3 minutes. Stir through tomato paste and tinned tomatoes. Reduce heat to a simmer and cook, uncovered, for 10–12 minutes.
3. Add olive oil and butter to a large non-stick frying pan and heat to high. Add meatballs, in batches, and, turning occasionally, cook until golden. Repeat until all meatballs are cooked. Return meatballs to the pan and then pour rich tomato sauce over the meatballs and simmer for 10–15 minutes.
4. Place the couscous into a large heatproof bowl and pour over 400 ml (14 fl oz) boiling water. Stir through butter, cover with plastic wrap and leave for 10 minutes. Fluff with a fork and season, to taste.
5. Divide cous cous between bowls, top with meatballs and tomato sauce. Add a dollop of Greek yogurt and scatter with cilantro. Serve immediately.

BRAISED BEEF CHEEKS IN AROMATIC ASIAN SPICES

with celeriac puree

Beef cheeks, (you guessed it, the facial muscles of a cow), are a secondary cut of meat, therefore they need to be cooked at a low temperature for a long time in order to produce a tender and delicious result. Most good butchers will have beef cheeks—you may just need to order them in advance. If you can't get cheek, you can also use beef shin—just chop it into even-size pieces.

INGREDIENTS

1 kg (2 lb) beef cheeks, trimmed
3 tablespoons kecap manis (Indonesian sweet soy
  sauce)
2 tablespoons rice bran oil (or any neutral oil)
3 garlic cloves, peeled and finely chopped
2 cm (¾ inch) piece fresh ginger, peeled and sliced
1 dried chili, whole
3 star anise
1 cinnamon stick
2 tablespoons fish sauce
1 tablespoon light palm sugar, grated
100 ml (3½ oz) Shaoxing rice wine

400 ml (14 fl oz) good quality chicken stock, salt
  reduced
2 sprigs mint
2 sprigs cilantro (coriander)

Celeriac puree

1 celeriac (about 500 g/1 lb 1½ oz), peeled and cut
  into 1 cm (½ inch) pieces
500 ml (16 fl oz) full cream milk
100 g (3½ oz) unsalted butter
pinch salt

METHOD

1. Place beef cheeks in a bowl. Pour kecap manis over cheeks and rub to coat. Place oil in a large saucepan over medium heat. Sear beef cheeks until lightly golden on all sides. Work in batches making sure you don't overcrowd the pan. Be careful, kecap manis burns quite easily. Turn heat down if this happens. Remove cheeks from the pan and set aside.
2. Add garlic and ginger to the same saucepan and cook until lightly golden. Stir through dried chili, star anise, cinnamon, fish sauce, palm sugar, Shaoxing wine and chicken stock. Return cheeks to the saucepan, bring to the boil, then reduce heat to a simmer. Cover and cook for 2 hours or until the meat is tender when pierced with a fork. Remove cheeks from the saucepan and set aside. To reduce the sauce for serving, increase the heat to medium and cook for a further 25–30 minutes. If you've made this the day before, when it cools, scrape off the layer of fat before reheating.
3. While the beef is cooking, prepare the celeriac. Place the diced celeriac in a saucepan and add the milk. Bring to the boil over medium heat, then reduce to a gentle simmer. Cover and, stirring occasionally, cook for 30 minutes or until the celeriac is soft. Drain, reserving the cooking liquid. Place celeriac in a food processor with butter and blend until smooth, adding the reserved cooking liquid, as required. Before serving, return cheeks to the reduced sauce and heat through.
4. Divide puree between bowls and top with beef cheeks and sauce. Scatter with mint and cilantro and serve immediately.

FILIPINO CHICKEN ADOBO

The key to the Philippines' national dish (adobo) is getting the right balance of sweetness, saltiness and acidity–cooking softens the sharpness of the vinegar while the aromatics (star anise and bay leaves) builds the complexity of the broth. I have used apple cider vinegar, which is full of enzymes, potassium, aids digestion and is great for the immune system.

INGREDIENTS

60 ml (2 fl oz) rice bran oil
1 kg (2 lb) or 4 chicken Marylands, skin on
sea salt and freshly ground black pepper
8 garlic cloves, peeled and crushed
2 cm (¾ inch) fresh ginger, grated
10 scallions (spring onions), cut into 4 cm (1½ inch)
  batons
1 star anise

4 dry bay leaves
1 dried red chili, whole
250 ml (8 fl oz) apple cider vinegar
75 ml (3 fl oz) tamari
175 ml (6 fl oz) good quality store-bought or
  Homemade Chicken Stock (pg 182)
2 long red chilies, deseeded and thinly sliced

METHOD

1. Heat the oil in a large frying pan to medium-high and oil is smoking. Season chicken with sea salt and pepper before sealing each Maryland for 6–8 minutes, or until browned on all sides. Add the garlic and ginger and cook for a further 1–2 minutes or until lightly golden. Stir in the scallions, star anise, bay leaves, dried chili, vinegar, tamari and stock. Bring to the boil and then reduce heat to low. Cover and cook for 30 minutes, or until chicken is tender and falling off the bone.
2. Serve with Steamed Coconut and Kaffir Lime Rice (pg 184) and garnish each bowl with red chili.

SPICY CUMIN LAMB
with flat rice noodles

Forget takeaway, this is quick to make and tasty to boot. This fiery marinade works a treat with strips of stir-fried lamb and slightly charred fresh rice noodles.

INGREDIENTS

Marinated lamb
1 tablespoon cumin seeds
1 tablespoon coriander seeds
1 tablespoon Sichuan peppercorns
2 garlic cloves, peeled and finely chopped
1 teaspoon fresh ginger, finely grated
2 tablespoons tamari
2 tablespoons Shaoxing rice wine
1 tablespoon sesame oil
1 teaspoon sea salt
6 dried red chilies, left whole
500 g (1 lb) boneless leg of lamb, cut into strips

Rice noodle
60 ml (2 fl oz) peanut oil
1 brown onion, peeled and sliced lengthways into strips
½ red bell pepper (capsicum), cut into 3 cm (1¼ inch) x 1 cm (½ inch) strips
8 scallions (spring onions), cut into 3 cm (1¼ inch) lengths
400 g (14 oz) fresh flat rice noodles*

*You can use dried rice noodles cooked according to packet instructions.

METHOD

1. In a mortar and pestle, coarsely grind the cumin seeds, coriander seeds and Sichuan peppercorns. Transfer ground spices to a large bowl and add the garlic, ginger, tamari, Shaoxing, sesame oil, salt and dried red chilies. Add the lamb strips and toss to coat. Cover and allow to marinate for at least 1 hour or overnight in the refrigerator.
2. Heat a wok with half the peanut oil until smoke appears. Add the onion and bell pepper and stir-fry until lightly golden. Add the scallions and cook until the edges are golden too. Remove and set aside.
3. Heat the remaining peanut oil in the same wok. Add the lamb and stir-fry until lamb is lightly golden and just cooked, about 1 minute. Toss in rice noodles and cook until the edges are slightly charred, about 3–4 minutes.
4. Return the onion, bell pepper and scallions to the wok. Toss to combine and serve immediately.

Shaoxing rice wine and fresh flat rice noodles are available from Asian supermarkets.

MAPLE BOURBON PORK BELLY BITES
with sweet potato and ginger mash

This sticky, rich maple bourbon braised pork belly is phenomenal and I can't tell you how many times people have asked for the recipe. Cooking pork belly can sometimes be a somewhat laborious process however, in this recipe, I've tried to simplify it (there's no skin so you don't have to worry about the crackling)—without jeopardising the end result.

INGREDIENTS

Pork belly bites
60 ml (2 fl oz) rice bran oil
1 kg (2 lb) lean pork belly, skin removed, cut into 3 cm (1¼ inch) cubes
5 garlic cloves, peeled and chopped
250 ml (8 fl oz) bourbon whisky
125 ml (4 fl oz) malt vinegar
125 ml (4 fl oz) kecap manis (Indonesian sweet soy sauce)
500 ml (16 fl oz) Homemade Chicken Stock (pg 180) or salt-reduced store-bought
250 ml (8 fl oz) pure maple syrup
1 star anise
4 bay leaves

Sweet potato and ginger mash
800 g (1 lb 12 oz) sweet potato, peeled and cut into 2 cm (¾ inch) to 3 cm (1¼ inch) pieces
1 tablespoon ginger, peeled and chopped
1 teaspoon sea salt
60 g (2 oz) butter
freshly ground pepper

Garnish
fresh cilantro (coriander) leaves
1 long red chili, de-seeded, cut lengthways in strips

METHOD

1. Preheat oven to 200°C (400°F).
2. Heat oil in a large, heavy-based saucepan to medium-high. Cook pork, in batches, turning regularly, until browned and crisp. As the pork is quite fatty, it will spit so have anti-splatter screen guard ready. Transfer to a bowl and repeat with remaining batches until all the pork is browned. Set pork aside and drain excess fat from the pan.
3. Using the same saucepan, add garlic and cook, stirring constantly, until lightly golden and fragrant. Stir through bourbon whisky, vinegar, kecap manis, stock, maple syrup, star anise and bay leaves and bring to the boil. Cook, stirring occasionally, for 10 minutes or until thickened slightly.
4. Return pork belly to the saucepan. Reduce heat to low, cover and simmer for 1½ hours or until pork is tender.
5. Meanwhile, to make the mash, place sweet potato, ginger and sea salt in a saucepan and add enough cold water so the vegetables are not quite covered. Bring to the boil and then reduce heat to low and cook, uncovered, for 20 minutes or until sweet potato is soft when pierced. Stir through butter, then using a heavy whisk, food processor or hand blender, stir or puree until smooth. Taste and season accordingly.
6. Take pork out of braise and continue to cook the sauce for a further 25–30 minutes or until the sauce has reduced by half.
7. Divide sweet potato mash between bowls, top with pork belly bites and drizzle with sauce. Scatter with cilantro and chili.

HUGHIE'S LASAGNA

A family recipe is important, even if we don't remember the exact method because each attempt at its re-creation keeps us connected to the people who helped shape us. This is one of those recipes, filled with love for my family. I have vivid memories of arriving home to the farm, exhausted and cold, to be greeted with the aromas of Mum's lasagna. My brother, Hugh loved this dish.

INGREDIENTS

6 large instant lasagna sheets
50 g (2 oz) mozzarella (or cheddar cheese)

Beef ragu

750 g (1 lb 8 oz) beef mince
2 tablespoons olive oil
2 brown onions, peeled and finely diced
2 garlic cloves, peeled and finely chopped
¼ teaspoon dried oregano

400 g (14 oz) tinned tomato soup
60 ml (2 fl oz) red wine (optional)
salt and freshly ground pepper

Béchamel

40 g (1½ oz) butter
40 g (1½ oz) all purpose (plain) flour
640 ml (22½ fl oz) milk

METHOD

1. Preheat oven to 180ºC (350°F).
2. To make the beef ragu, heat oil in a medium saucepan to high. Add onions and garlic and cook until lightly golden. Add mince and stir regularly to brown the meat. Sprinkle with oregano, a pinch of salt and some freshly ground black pepper. Add tomato soup and red wine. Cover and simmer for 45 minutes, stirring occasionally.
3. Meanwhile, to prepare the béchamel, melt butter in a small saucepan over medium-low heat. Add the flour and stir continuously for 1 minute (to cook the flour), then remove saucepan from the heat. Using a whisk, pour a small amount of the milk into the flour mixture and mix to combine. Add the remaining milk, a little at a time, stirring continuously, until it is all combined. Return the pan to the heat and, stirring continuously, cook for a further 8 minutes or until the sauce thickens. Remove from the heat.
4. To assemble the lasagna, lightly grease a 30 cm x 20 cm (12 inch x 8 inch) ceramic baking dish with butter. Pour about 250 g (9 oz) of the ragu into the baking dish.
5. Arrange 2 pasta sheets in a single layer over the ragu and then cover with another layer of the ragu. Top with béchamel sauce and then repeat layering the pasta, ragu and béchamel until you have 3 layers of pasta, finishing with béchamel on top. Sprinkle with mozzarella or cheddar cheese.
6. Bake in the oven for 45–50 minutes or until cooked through. You can test if it is cooked by pricking the lasagna with a fork. If the fork pushes through easily, it is done. Let the lasagna stand for 5 minutes before serving.

RED DUCK CURRY

with lychees and Thai basil

This recipe is a labor of love but one you won't regret. This is one of my mum's favorite dishes and I think she'd eat it every night if she could. Duck Marylands are sometimes tricky to find—if you can, get your butcher to order them in. This is a great dinner party recipe because you can do absolutely everything ahead of time so you won't have to lift a finger.

INGREDIENTS

Red curry paste

5 dried red chilies
1 teaspoon shrimp paste
1 teaspoon coriander seeds
½ teaspoon cumin seeds
1 teaspoon white peppercorns
2 cilantro (coriander) roots, cleaned and chopped
1 red Asian shallot (eschalot), peeled and roughly chopped
4 garlic cloves, peeled and roughly chopped
1 lemongrass stalk, finely sliced
½ tablespoon galangal
zest of 1 lime, about ½ tablespoon (can substitute lemon zest)
1 teaspoon salt

Curry

2 tablespoons duck fat (or peanut oil)
4 duck Marylands (legs), skin on
3 tablespoons red curry paste (above)
500 ml (16 fl oz) tinned coconut milk, unshaken or chilled in the refrigerator for a few hours
2 tablespoons gluten free fish sauce
2 tablespoons light palm sugar
6 kaffir lime leaves, stem removed and thinly sliced
2 large red chilies, halved and deseeded
12 lychees, halved and stoned
12 cherry tomatoes
60 g (2 oz) Thai basil leaves (or regular basil leaves)

METHOD

1. Preheat oven to 180°C (350°F).
2. For the curry paste, soak the chilies in hot water for 30 minutes. Remove from water and finely chop. Next, wrap the shrimp paste in foil and roast in the oven for 10 minutes or until dry and crumbly.
3. In a frying pan, dry roast coriander seeds and cumin seeds until fragrant, about 2 minutes. Transfer to a mortar and pestle, together with white peppercorns and grind to a rough powder. Place in a food processor and add the remaining red curry paste ingredients. Process to a smooth paste. Set aside 3 tablespoons of curry paste and transfer remaining paste to an airtight jar. Curry paste will keep for up to 2 weeks or freeze for up to 2 months.
4. Add duck fat to a large ovenproof frying pan or casserole dish over medium heat. Add the duck, skin side down, and cook, turning once, until lightly golden all over. Remove from the pan. Add the curry paste and cook for few minutes until fragrant.
5. Open the tin of coconut milk and, using a spoon, scoop off the hardened coconut "cream". Reserve the remaining milk. Add to the curry paste and cook for 3–5 minutes or until the cream starts to separate and bubble. Stir in the remaining coconut milk, fish sauce, palm sugar and kaffir lime. Return duck to the pan. Cover with foil or a tight fitting lid. Cook in the oven for 1½ hours or until the meat comes away from the bone. Five minutes prior to serving, add chilies, lychees and tomatoes.
6. Garnish with Thai basil leaves. Serve with Steamed Jasmine Rice (pg 185).

JAMAICAN JERK CHICKEN
with charred corn salad and honey mustard dressing

Jerk chicken—fragrant, fiery and smoky—is a dish for which Jamaica is justly famous. The charred corn, chili and avocado salad, dressed with a honey mustard vinaigrette is a delicious accompaniment. My dear friend Liz, who is an extremely talented cook, tested the recipe and gave me her glowing approval (phew!) but she recommended serving with Tabasco, which I've included here.

INGREDIENTS
Jerk chicken
1 tablespoon ground allspice

1 tablespoon dried thyme leaves

2 teaspoons black peppercorns, freshly ground

1 teaspoon ground coriander

1 teaspoon ground cinnamon

1 teaspoon paprika

½ teaspoon ground nutmeg

½ teaspoon ground chili

5 garlic cloves, peeled and finely chopped

4 small red chilies, deseeded and finely chopped

1 cm (½ inch) fresh ginger, finely grated

2 tablespoons olive oil

2 tablespoons lemon juice

2 tablespoons tamari

100 ml (3½ oz) orange juice (about 1 fresh orange, juiced)

750 g (1 lb 8 oz) chicken thigh fillets (about 4), skin removed, cut into 2 cm x 10 cm (¾ inch x 4 inch) pieces

Charred Corn Salad with Honey Mustard Dressing (pg 133)

METHOD
1. To make the jerk paste, place all the ingredients in a food processor or mortar and pestle and blend to a smooth paste. Combine with chicken in a large non-reactive bowl. Toss to coat, cover and refrigerate for at least 2 hours or overnight.
2. Make the Charred Corn Salad with Honey Mustard Dressing (pg 133).
3. Heat a grill pan or barbecue to high. Add oil and when the pan or grill is hot, cook chicken, turning and basting occasionally with the marinade, until just cooked through. Cover with foil and set aside to rest for a few minutes. Serve with the Charred Corn Salad and Tabasco sauce (if desired).

LAMB RUMP

with spring bean salad

Paired with seared, still-pink lamb this salad bursts with spring flavors. As always, fresh is best so don't feel as though you need to use all the different types of beans—use what is in season. Broad bean seeds have a tough outer skin and many people make the mistake of boiling the beans until these skins soften, which makes the beans mushy.

INGREDIENTS

4 x 250 g (9 oz) lamb rump, at room temperature
sea salt and freshly ground pepper
2 tablespoons olive oil

100 g (3½ oz) black (Kalamata) olives, pitted and torn
  in half
½ bunch (small) mint leaves

Spring bean salad
4 runner beans, trimmed, halved (optional)
12 snow peas, topped and tailed
12 asparagus spears, woody ends trimmed
8 fresh broad beans (or use 120 g/4 oz frozen)
60 g (2 oz) Danish fetta, roughly chopped

Vinaigrette
60 ml (2 fl oz) olive oil
2 tablespoons white wine vinegar
1 lemon, zest and juice
sea salt and freshly ground pepper

METHOD

1. Preheat oven to 180°C (350°F).
2. To prepare salad, start by prepping your beans. For the runner beans, use a vegetable peeler to remove the string that runs up both sides of the bean and then slice, on an angle, into strips. For the snow peas, top and tail and remove the outer string and slice, on the angle, into strips. For the broad beans, remove each bean from their pods.
3. Bring a large saucepan of salted water to the boil. Add the runner beans and cook for a maximum of 1 minute. Use a slotted spoon to remove. Drain and set aside. Next, add snow peas and asparagus. Cook for 1 minute. Remove, drain well and then dry the asparagus with a clean kitchen towel. Lastly, cook the broad beans for 2–3 minutes. Plunge into ice cold water to stop the cooking process. Drain and remove beans from their inner pods and set aside.
4. To prepare dressing, combine olive oil, vinegar, lemon zest and juice, salt and pepper.
5. Season the lamb liberally with salt and pepper. Heat oil in a heavy frying pan to medium-high. Place lamb rump on pan and cook on all sides until brown.
6. Place on a baking tray and transfer to the oven for 10 minutes. At this point, you can use a meat thermometer and check if it is at 51°C.
7. Once all the beans are cooked and cooled, combine in a large bowl. Add Danish fetta, olives and mint, pour the dressing over and toss to combine.
8. Allow the lamb to rest for 10 minutes before slicing and serving on top of the spring bean salad.

SWEET SPICED DUCK MARYLANDS
with chili and plums

I was having a bit of fun when I made up this dish, I wasn't sure if I was in the Middle East or Asia. Either way, I love the rustic flavors in this deceptively simple braise. The sweet spices accentuate the duck's natural richness and the plums break down during cooking, creating a thick sauce, speckled with chili.

INGREDIENTS

Spice rub
1 teaspoon ground cinnamon
1 teaspoon ground cumin
1 teaspoon ground coriander
1 teaspoon sea salt, or to taste
¼ teaspoon freshly ground black pepper
2 tablespoons olive oil

Braised duck
4 duck Marylands (legs and thighs), skin on
2 fresh red chilies, de-seeded, thinly sliced lengthways (into strips)
5 star anise
500 ml (16 fl oz) good-quality chicken stock
8 plums, halved and de-stoned

METHOD

1. To make the spice rub, combine spices in a bowl, large enough to fit the duck Marylands. Add 1 tablespoon of the oil to make a paste. Massage the spice paste into the duck pieces, coating each Maryland. Cover and refrigerate for at least 1 hour or overnight, if time permits.

2. Heat the remaining 1 tablespoon olive oil in a large, heavy-based saucepan on medium-high. Brown the duck pieces, turning so they brown evenly. Lower the heat and add the chili, star anise and stock. Arrange the halved plums under and around the duck pieces, packing the plums firmly around the duck. Cover and simmer for 1½ hours, or until the duck is very tender. If you're extremely organized and have made this the day before, when the sauce cools, scrape off the layer of fat that formed before you reheat. Save the duck fat to make Sweet Potato Wedges (pg 79)—the spices that the duck are cooked in make the sweet potatoes even more delicious.

3. Serve as part of a banquet with Steamed Jasmine Rice (pg 185) and Stir-fried Green Beans with Honey and Miso (pg 144).

If plums aren't in season, they can be replaced with apples, pears or peaches.

GRILLED LAMB CUTLETS
with eggplant caponata and salsa verde

These lamb cutlets, simply grilled, work delightfully with this Sicilian sweet and sour caponata. Salsa verde, the classic green colored condiment of Italy, is a very versatile sauce—it adds a lively freshness to almost any dish. I often substitute the lamb with swordfish skewers, which makes a great alternative to red meat.

INGREDIENTS

Rosemary lamb cutlets
8 small lamb cutlets, French trimmed
1 sprig rosemary leaves
1 tablespoon extra virgin olive oil
sea salt and freshly ground pepper

Caponata
3 tablespoons extra virgin olive oil
1 large Spanish onion, peeled and finely diced
2 garlic cloves, peeled and finely chopped
1 large eggplant (aubergine), cut into 1 cm (½ inch) cubes
1 large bell pepper (red capsicum), cut into 1 cm (½ inch) cubes
4 tablespoons red wine vinegar
3 tablespoons water

1 tablespoon brown sugar
2 tablespoons sultanas
1 tablespoon lemon juice
1 tablespoon pine nuts

Salsa verde
1 bunch flat-leaf parsley, roughly chopped
1 bunch basil, roughly chopped
2 anchovy fillets, roughly chopped
1 teaspoon baby capers
1 garlic clove, peeled and roughly chopped
1 tablespoon extra virgin olive oil
1 tablespoon lemon juice, to taste
½ tablespoon red wine vinegar
sea salt and freshly ground pepper, to taste

METHOD

1. Place the lamb cutlets in a shallow dish. Sprinkle with rosemary and extra virgin olive oil. Season generously with salt and pepper. Cover and leave to marinate for a minimum of 20 minutes.
2. To make the caponata, heat a frying pan to medium-high and add oil. Stir through onion and cook for 3 minutes or until softened. Add the garlic and cook for a further minute. Add eggplant and bell pepper and cook, stirring, for 4 minutes or until lightly golden and softened, adding a little more oil, if necessary. Stir in remaining ingredients, and cook for 5 minutes or until liquid has evaporated. Set aside.
3. To make the salsa verde, place all ingredients in a food processor and blend until it reaches a smooth consistency. Taste and adjust lemon juice accordingly.
4. Heat a large frying pan to medium-high. Remove the lamb from the marinade and cook, in batches for 2–3 minutes on each side, depending on the size of the cutlets. You want the meat to be pink in the middle. Cover with foil and allow to rest for 5 minutes.
5. Divide caponata between bowls and place two lamb cutlets on top. Serve with salsa verde, to the side, or on top.

CHARRED LAMB SKEWERS
with quinoa tabbouleh and tzatziki

These lamb skewers are served at every family barbeque we have–and I've never met anyone who doesn't love them. My take on a traditional bulghur tabbouleh, this quinoa version is a great alternative for those who can't tolerate wheat.

INGREDIENTS

750 g (1 lb 8 oz) boned leg of lamb, cut into 2 cm (¾ inch) cubes
2 tablespoons peanut oil
1 tablespoon tamari
1 tablespoon lemon juice
3 garlic cloves, peeled and finely chopped
1 teaspoon finely grated ginger
1 teaspoon ground turmeric
1 teaspoon ground coriander
1 teaspoon ground cumin
10 dried curry leaves, crushed
sea salt and freshly ground black pepper

Quinoa tabbouleh
200 g (7 oz) white quinoa, rinsed and drained

500 ml (16 fl oz) water
250 g (9 oz) punnet cherry tomatoes, quartered
2 bunches continental (curly) parsley, washed, dried and finely chopped
1 bunch mint leaves, roughly chopped
3 scallions (spring onions), thinly sliced
½ Spanish onion, peeled and fined diced
125 ml (4 fl oz) olive oil
juice of 2 lemons

Tzatziki
½ large cucumber
1 teaspoon salt
200 g (7 oz) gluten free Greek yogurt
1 garlic clove, peeled and grated on a microplane

METHOD

1. Soak 8 long bamboo skewers in cold water for 30 minutes.
2. Combine all the ingredients for the marinade in a non-reactive bowl. Add lamb and toss to combine making sure the lamb is coated with the marinade. Refrigerate for at least 2 hours or for up to 3 days (the longer the better).
3. For the tabbouleh, start by cooking the quinoa. In a small saucepan, combine the quinoa and water. Bring to the boil and then cover. Reduce the heat and cook until the liquid has been absorbed and the quinoa is tender, about 15 minutes. Uncover, fluff the quinoa with a fork and transfer to a large bowl. Allow to cool before adding the remaining tabbouleh ingredients. Toss to combine and set aside.
4. For the tzatziki, grate the cucumber and place in a fine mesh sieve, set over a bowl. Sprinkle with salt and allow to drain for at least 15 minutes. Discard drained water and squeeze cucumber to remove any excess liquid. Place in a small bowl and stir through yogurt and garlic until combined.
5. When ready to cook, thread lamb onto bamboo skewers. Heat char-grill pan or barbeque to medium-high and char lamb until just cooked, about 2–3 minutes. Alternatively, you can cook the lamb skewers under a hot grill.
6. Divide tabouleh between four serving bowls. Use a fork to push the meat off each skewer and divide between bowls. Serve with a dollop of tzatziki and Roasted Garlic Hummus (pg 31).

VEGETARIAN

Vegetarianism is a growing trend in today's health-conscious society. With studies and scientific research constantly making headlines revealing the impact of processed food on our health, it's no wonder many people are making a transition to a more wholesome, and even vegetarian diet. The older I get, the more I tend to lean towards a plant-based diet. Don't get me wrong, there'll always be a place for roast chicken on a Sunday night but on a daily basis, I enjoy veg-centric meals.

I must point out that a vegetarian meal needn't be comprised exclusively of vegetables. Hearty whole grains make up the base of many of my vegetarian bowls and I like to top the dish off with protein-packed tofu or a handful of nuts and seeds. Colorful, vibrant and tasty dishes sing out on every page of this chapter which I hope will inspire even the most carnivorous of you to enjoy a meat-free day or two.

If you're craving something quick and healthy cue my umami-rich Caramelized Miso Tofu (pg 109) with a herbaceous glass noodle and edamame salad. Alternatively, for a rainbow-colored dish, try the visually appealing and super tasty Falafel-spiced Chickpeas with Red Cabbage and Nashi Pear Slaw with Lemon Tahini Dressing (pg 113). The first time my husband decided that he loved tofu (shhhh, don't tell his mates) was when I cooked the Black Pepper Tofu, Portobello Mushrooms with Vermicelli Noodles (pg 111). It may not look particularly pretty but it's tasty. This dish, in particular, will convert even the most hard-core meat lovers.

ROASTED SWEET POTATO SKINS

with creamy cashew dressing

All hail the sweet potato—roasted, mashed, steamed, fried, grilled or grated—to me, those orange-fleshed spuds are the ultimate comfort food. When you roast sweet potatoes whole, remember to poke a few holes in the skin as they've been known to explode in the oven (it's not only messy but dangerous).

INGREDIENTS

4 small orange sweet potatoes, about 1½ kg (3 lb) total
2 tablespoons olive oil
sea salt and freshly ground pepper

Creamy cashew dressing

3 tablespoons raw cashew nuts
1 garlic clove, peeled and roughly chopped
1 tablespoon tamari

2 teaspoons sesame oil
1 teaspoon ginger, finely grated
2 tablespoons lime juice (or lemon juice)

Toppings

2 tablespoons pine nuts, dry roasted
2 scallions (spring onions), thinly sliced
½ bunch cilantro (coriander) leaves
½ bunch mint leaves

METHOD

1. Preheat oven to 180°C (350°F).
2. Pierce sweet potatoes with a skewer or fork and place on a baking tray. Bake for 55– 60 minutes or until tender when pierced with a skewer. Remove from the oven and allow to cool slightly.
3. While the sweet potatoes are cooking, prepare the creamy cashew dressing. In a frying pan, dry roast the cashews for 2 minutes or until lightly golden. Place in a food processor with the remaining ingredients and blend until combined. Add 3–4 tablespoons water, if necessary, to reach a thick but pourable consistency.
4. Once sweet potatoes are cooked, slice in half lengthways and use a spoon to carefully scoop out about half of the flesh. Set aside the removed flesh (you can use this to make Sweet Potato and Ginger Mash (pg 92).
5. Preheat oven grill. Brush sweet potato skins with 2 tablespoons olive oil and season with salt and pepper. Place sweet potatoes under a grill and cook for a further 8–10 minutes or until golden and crisp.
6. Drizzle over Thai cashew sauce and scatter with pine nuts, scallions, coriander and mint. Serve immediately.

CARAMELIZED MISO TOFU

with edamame and asparagus glass noodles

From the caramelized, nutty-flavored tofu and soft crunch of the edamame beans to the silky bite of the glass noodle and fresh herbs, this dish is a contrast of textures and tastes. It's important to drain the noodles well otherwise the excess water will dilute the punchiness of the dressing. There are lots of types of miso. I prefer white (shiro) miso as it's lighter and sweeter.

INGREDIENTS

Miso tofu

1½ tablespoons white (shiro) miso paste

2 tablespoons tamari

2 teaspoons pure maple syrup

1 teaspoon sesame oil

¼ teaspoon freshly ground black pepper

375 g (13 oz) firm, fresh tofu, drained, patted dry and cut into thick rectangles

1 tablespoon rice bran oil

Edamame, asparagus and glass noodle salad

400 g (14 oz) glass (also called cellophane or mung bean) noodles

200 g (7 oz) cooked edamame beans, podded

16 asparagus spears, woody ends removed and cut on the diagonal into 3 cm (1¼ inch) pieces

4 scallions (spring onions), white part only, finely chopped

1 bunch cilantro (coriander) leaves

1 bunch mint leaves

1 tablespoon white sesame seeds, toasted

Dressing

2 garlic cloves, peeled and finely grated on a microplane

1 cm (½ inch) ginger, finely grated

4 tablespoons fresh lime juice

2 tablespoons peanut oil

2 tablespoons tamari

2 teaspoons sesame oil

2 tablespoons honey

2 long red chilies, deseeded and thinly sliced

METHOD

1. Prepare the tofu marinade by whisking together the miso, tamari, maple syrup, sesame oil and pepper in a shallow bowl. Add tofu rectangles to the marinade, toss to coat, cover with plastic wrap and set aside until you are ready to cook.
2. Pour boiling water over your noodles and leave for 5–10 minutes or until softened. Drain water and set aside.
3. Bring a medium saucepan of water to the boil. Add edamame beans and asparagus. Blanch for 20 seconds. Remove, drain and allow to cool.
4. In a large bowl, combine the glass noodles, edamame, asparagus, scallions, herbs and sesame seeds.
5. In another bowl, whisk to combine all the dressing ingredients. Set aside.
6. Heat rice bran oil in a grill (griddle) pan to high. Add tofu pieces, in batches, and cook until char-grilled. Set aside and continue until all the tofu is cooked.
7. Just before serving, pour dressing over salad and toss to combine. Divide salad between serving bowls and top with warm, char-grilled tofu. Serve immediately.

CREAMY GREEN SOUP
with toasted coconut

Soup is a great way to use up any leftover greens—here we combine broccoli and leek to create a virtuous green soup, which can be on the table in less than 30 minutes. When I'm feeling run down and exhausted, this garlic-loaded soup is my go-to dish.

INGREDIENTS

2 tablespoons olive oil
1 brown onion, peeled and finely diced
1 leek (white part only), thinly sliced
5 garlic cloves, peeled and finely chopped
½ teaspoon dried chili flakes
500 ml (16 fl oz) good quality vegetable stock
800 g (1 lb 12 oz) or 2 heads of broccoli, cut into
    smaller florets, stalk sliced

1 x 400 ml (14 fl oz) tinned coconut milk
1 tablespoon tamari
sea salt and freshly ground pepper

Toasted coconut
2 tablespoons shredded coconut
¼ teaspoon sea salt

METHOD

1. Heat oil in a large saucepan to medium-high. Add onion and leek and sauté until tender. Stir through garlic and dried chili flakes and cook until garlic is lightly golden.
2. Add stock and broccoli florets and bring to the boil. Reduce heat, cover and simmer for 20 minutes or until broccoli is tender when pierced with a fork.
3. Meanwhile, make the toasted coconut by heating a non-stick frying pan to medium. Add the coconut and sea salt and distribute evenly across the bottom of the pan. Stir frequently as the coconut tends to crisp and turn brown pretty quickly. Cook until lightly golden and remove from the pan immediately. (Alternatively, you can buy already-toasted coconut). Set aside.
4. Once broccoli is tender, remove from the heat. Stir through coconut milk and tamari, then process with a hand-held blender until smooth.
5. Divide between four bowls and scatter with toasted coconut.

BLACK PEPPER TOFU, PORTOBELLO MUSHROOMS

with vermicelli noodles

On its own, tofu can be fairly bland and unexciting. Pan-fried until golden, with a crisp-chewy crust, tossed with caramelized mushrooms and a robust, peppery, sweet sauce, tofu becomes something so delicious you'll keep going back for more. Portobello mushrooms have a meaty texture that holds its own in this stir-fry but you can easily substitute with oyster mushrooms which release a nutty taste sensation when cooked.

INGREDIENTS

2 large Portobello mushroom caps (or oyster mushrooms)

375 g (13 oz) firm, fresh tofu, drained and patted dry

4 tablespoons rice bran oil

4 scallions (spring onions), cut into segments about 3 cm (1¼ inch) lengths

1 long red chili, deseeded and thinly sliced

4 garlic cloves, peeled and crushed

1 teaspoon freshly grated ginger

1 tablespoon whole black peppercorns

1 tablespoon tamarind puree

2 tablespoons kecap manis (Indonesian sweet soy sauce)

1 tablespoon tamari

2 teaspoons pure maple syrup (or sugar)

½ teaspoon sesame oil

60 ml (2 fl oz) good quality vegetable stock

250 g (9 oz) dried rice vermicelli noodles, soaked in boiling water for 3–4 minutes (or until softened), then drained well

METHOD

1. Prepare mushrooms by brushing off any dirt and trimming the hard end of each stem. Halve caps and then slice crosswise into slices. Set aside. If using oyster mushrooms, separate the mushrooms into individual caps. Brush off any dirt around the base of the mushroom and trim the rough end. Tear into bite-size pieces.

2. Cut the tofu into ½ cm (¼ inch) thick rectangles. Heat half the rice bran oil in a heavy-based saucepan to medium-high. Shallow fry the tofu in batches making sure not to crowd the pan. Turn the pieces as you go. Once they are golden and crunchy on all sides, transfer to a plate and continue until all the tofu is done, adding more oil if necessary.

3. In the same saucepan, heat the remaining (2 tablespoons) oil and sauté the mushrooms, scallions, chilies, garlic and ginger. Cook for 5–10 minutes on low-medium heat, stirring occasionally, until the mushrooms are caramelized and soft.

4. Meanwhile, partially crush the peppercorns using a mortar and pestle.

5. Once the mushrooms are soft, add the remaining ingredients to the pan – ground black pepper, tamarind, kecap manis, tamari, maple syrup, sesame oil and stock. Cook for a few minutes or until sauce thickens slightly.

6. Return the tofu to the pan at the last minute and toss to combine.

7. Serve immediately with vermicelli noodles.

FALAFEL-SPICED CHICKPEAS

with red cabbage nashi pear slaw and lemon tahini dressing

These spiced chickpeas are the perfect match for coleslaw with a difference—it's crunchy, sweet, sour, savory and creamy all at once. The lemon-tahini dressing adds a creamy, nutty dimension to the dish and is a great recipe to have up your sleeve for all sorts of salads.

INGREDIENTS

2 tablespoons extra virgin olive oil
2 teaspoons ground cumin
2 teaspoons ground coriander
½ teaspoon salt
½ teaspoon paprika
2 x 400 g (14 oz) tinned chickpeas, drained and rinsed

Red cabbage and nashi pear slaw

2 tablespoons olive oil
150 g (5 oz) gluten free sour cream (or Greek yogurt)
2 tablespoons white wine vinegar
2 tablespoons lemon juice
1 garlic clove, peeled and crushed
sea salt and freshly ground pepper

½ red cabbage, finely shredded
1 nashi pear, unpeeled, cored and julienned
1 small Spanish onion, peeled and thinly sliced lengthways
3 red or watermelon radishes, thinly sliced
2 scallions (spring onions), thinly sliced
½ bunch flat-leaf parsley, roughly chopped
½ bunch mint, roughly chopped

Lemon tahini dressing

2 tablespoons hulled tahini
1 tablespoon lemon juice
2 tablespoons cold water
¼ teaspoon salt

METHOD

1. Preheat oven to 200°C (400°F).
2. In a medium bowl, combine oil, cumin, coriander, salt and paprika. Using paper towel, pat chickpeas dry and then add to the spices. Toss to completely coat the chickpeas, then spread evenly on a tray lined with baking (parchment) paper. Transfer to the oven and roast until golden for 20–25 minutes, tossing occasionally. Set aside.
3. Meanwhile, to make the coleslaw, combine oil, sour cream (or yogurt), vinegar, lemon juice, garlic, salt and pepper in a large bowl and whisk until smooth and combined. Add red cabbage, pear, Spanish onion, radish and scallions and toss to combine. Just before serving, toss in herbs.
4. For the dressing, whisk together the tahini and lemon juice in a medium bowl. Add the water, a little at a time, until it reaches a creamy but pourable consistency. You may need to add more water, depending on the thickness of your tahini. Season with salt.
5. Divide slaw between bowls, scatter with roasted chickpeas and drizzle with dressing.

ROASTED BEETROOT RISOTTO
with fetta and mint

Risottos may have gone out of fashion but this dish is a showstopper, especially if you're a beetroot lover, like me. I have always preferred roasting beets (rather than boiling), as it tends to bring out the beet's sweeter side and the texture becomes silky and tender. Use arborio or carnaroli rice for the best results and check the use-by date—fresh rice is best.

INGREDIENTS

500 g (1 lb) fresh baby beetroot, trimmed
1 tablespoon olive oil
1.5 L (2½ pint) good quality vegetable stock (or chicken)
2 tablespoons unsalted butter
1 large brown onion, peeled and diced
4 garlic cloves, peeled and finely chopped
350 g (11½ oz) arborio (risotto) rice

2 sprigs fresh thyme
150 ml (5 fl oz) white wine
1 tablespoon lemon juice
60 g (2 oz) fresh Parmesan, freshly grated
100 g (3½ oz) Danish fetta, crumbed
2 sprigs mint leaves
sea salt and freshly ground black pepper

METHOD

1. Preheat oven to 200°C (400°F).
2. Wrap each beetroot bulb in foil. Spread on a baking tray and cook for 45–50 minutes or until tender. Check if cooked by piercing the beetroot with a skewer—no resistance means it's ready. Once cooked, allow to cool then use plastic gloves to peel the beetroot. Set half the beetroot aside at this point. Transfer the remaining half to a food processor and blend until it reaches a smooth consistency. You can add a tablespoon of stock if it doesn't combine.
3. Chop the set aside beetroot into thin wedges, drizzle with olive oil and place on a baking tray. Return to the oven and roast for a further 15–20 minutes or until caramelized around the edges. Keep warm and set aside to serve.
4. Pour the stock into a saucepan and bring to the boil then lower to a simmer.
5. In another large saucepan, melt butter over medium-low heat. Add onion and garlic. Stir regularly and cook for 3–5 minutes or until the onion softens and becomes translucent. Add the rice and stir to coat. Increase the heat and then add the wine, stirring constantly.
6. Once the rice has absorbed the wine, add a ladle of hot stock and throw in the thyme. Once the liquid has absorbed, add another ladle of stock and keep stirring. Repeat this process until you have used up all the stock and the rice is just about cooked, about 20 minutes. The rice shouldn't be mushy—it should have just a little 'bite' (*al dente*).
7. Stir though beetroot puree, lemon juice and Parmesan. Finally, fold through most of the Danish fetta, reserving a little fetta to serve. Divide between bowls, top with roasted beetroot wedges, reserved fetta and mint. Serve immediately.

ROAST PUMPKIN AND MISO SOUP
with tamari toasted seeds

I have a confession: I don't love pumpkin soup. This recipe, however, is an exception. Unlike many pumpkin soups, this one seems to take on a different personality with each mouthful—a hint of sweet miso, a chunk of sweet potato, a fleck of caramelized Spanish onion or a tang of ginger. I simply must talk about these tamari toasted seeds too—they're not only sublime sprinkled on this soup but also as a healthy snack—make a double batch, you won't regret it.

INGREDIENTS
1 kg (2 lb) butternut squash (butternut pumpkin)
500 g (1 lb) sweet potato
4 garlic cloves, peeled and finely chopped
3 tablespoons extra virgin olive oil, divided
sea salt
½ Spanish onion, peeled and finely diced
2 teaspoons fresh ginger, grated
2 tablespoons white (shiro) miso paste
1.5 L (2½ pints) good quality vegetable stock

1 tablespoon tamari
1 teaspoon sesame oil

Tamari toasted seeds
2 teaspoons extra virgin olive oil
2 tablespoons pumpkin seeds (pepitas)
2 tablespoons sunflower seeds
1 teaspoon tamari

METHOD
1. Preheat oven to 200°C (400°F).
2. Peel the squash and cut into 4 cm (1½ inch) x 2 cm (¾ inch) rectangles. Peel and cut the sweet potatoes into similar-sized pieces.
3. Line a large tray (or two) with baking (parchment) paper. Spread the squash, sweet potato and garlic in a single layer. Make sure the vegetables are not too crowded. Toss with 2 tablespoons of olive oil and sprinkle with salt. Roast for 30 minutes, tossing halfway through, or until the squash and sweet potato are cooked through.
4. Add the remaining 1 tablespoon of olive oil to a large saucepan over moderate heat. Add the onion and ginger and cook until softened. Add the miso, vegetable stock, tamari and sesame oil. Stir until combined. Add the roasted vegetables and simmer uncovered for 15 minutes.
5. Meanwhile, prepare the seeds. Heat a small frying pan to low. Add the olive oil, pumpkin and sunflower seeds and cook stirring regularly until lightly golden. Add the tamari and stir well to coat. Set aside.
6. Puree the soup using a stick blender or food processor, being careful not to over process the soup—it should still have a little texture. Divide the soup between bowls and scatter with tamari toasted seeds to serve.

HONEY AND OREGANO HALOUMI
with pearl barley

This epic dish combines honey-caramelized haloumi with a tart hint of lemon zest, chewy pearl barley and a scattering of fresh herbs. Made from sheep's milk, haloumi is a Greek cheese that has a high melting point that makes it perfect for grilling or pan-frying. Pearl barley is an often-overlooked grain that has a gorgeously chewy texture and a nutty taste.

INGREDIENTS

Pearl barley

1 tablespoon unsalted butter
2 teaspoons extra virgin olive oil
½ brown onion, peeled and diced
2 garlic cloves, peeled and finely chopped
300 g (10½ oz) pearl barley
800 ml (1½ pint) good quality vegetable stock
4 tablespoons fresh flat-leaf parsley, finely chopped

Honey and lemon haloumi

2 lemons, halved
1 tablespoon extra virgin olive oil
250 g (9 oz) haloumi, cut into 1 cm (½ inch) thick slices
2 tablespoons honey
4 sprigs oregano
1 teaspoon lemon zest

METHOD

1. To cook the barley, add the butter and olive oil to a saucepan over a medium heat. When bubbling, add the onion and garlic. Cook until the onion is just translucent. Add the pearl barley. Toss to coat and cook for a further 2–3 minutes stirring continuously. Pour in the stock and simmer, uncovered, until the barley is tender but retains a slight bite, about 35 minutes. Set aside. When ready to serve, stir through flat-leaf parsley.
2. Bring a grill pan or barbecue to medium heat. Place 4 lemon halves, cut side-down and cook until charred. Remove and set aside.
3. Add olive oil to a large frying pan and bring to medium-high heat. Add haloumi and cook for 2 minutes on each side or until golden. Drizzle honey around the haloumi and add oregano and lemon zest. Allow to bubble up and caramelize, about 2 minutes. Be careful not to let it burn.
4. Divide pearl barley between bowls. Top with haloumi and drizzle with any remaining sauce left in the pan. Serve each bowl with a char-grilled lemon half.

MISO GLAZED JAPANESE EGGPLANT
with scallion brown rice and broccolini

Known as nasu dengaku in Japan, I absolutely love miso eggplant. I always order it when I'm out for Japanese but they're incredibly easy to make at home. This recipe calls for long, skinny Japanese eggplants, also called finger or Lebanese eggplant, which are tender and sweet, but you could use the more common variety. Brown rice—higher in fiber than its white counterpart—is the perfect vehicle to carry this Japanese-inspired dish.

INGREDIENTS

Spring onion brown rice
280 g (9 oz) long-grain brown rice
3 scallions (spring onions), white part only, thinly
    chopped
1 tablespoon tamari
½ teaspoon sesame oil
1 cm (½ inch) ginger, grated on a microplane

Miso eggplant
6 Japanese eggplant (aubergine)*, about 500 g (1 lb)
1 tablespoon olive oil
sea salt, to taste
1 tablespoon white and black sesame seeds, toasted

Miso dressing
2 tablespoons white (shiro) miso paste
1 tablespoon mirin
2 teaspoons tamari (or light soy sauce)
2 teaspoons pure maple syrup (substitute agave
    nectar or sugar)
1 teaspoon sesame oil

Sautéed broccolini
1 tablespoon olive oil
2 bunches broccolini, woody ends removed
1 garlic clove, peeled and roughly chopped

METHOD
1. Preheat oven to 200°C (400°F).
2. Start by steaming your brown rice. Place rice, scallions, tamari, sesame oil and ginger in a medium saucepan. Add 500 ml (16 fl oz) water and bring to the boil. Reduce heat to low, cover and simmer until rice is just tender and water has evaporated, about 25–30 minutes. Set aside.
3. Meanwhile, slice your eggplants in half lengthways and lightly score the cut surfaces of the eggplant in a criss-cross pattern. Brush the cut side with olive oil and sprinkle with salt. Place on a tray lined with baking (parchment) paper, cut side up and roast for 10 minutes, or until the eggplant is lightly golden.
4. In a bowl, add miso, mirin, tamari, maple syrup and sesame oil and whisk to combine. Pour the miso dressing over semi-roasted eggplant. Return eggplant to the oven and roast for a further 10–15 minutes or until the miso caramelizes.
5. Add olive oil to a frying pan over medium heat. Add broccolini and sauté, tossing regularly, until broccolini is tender and just golden around the edges. Add garlic and cook until lightly golden.
6. Divide rice between bowls, top with broccolini and 3 eggplant halves per person. Scatter with toasted sesame seeds.

MAKE FRIENDS WITH SALAD

Growing up on a farm has given me a lifelong love for all things grown out of the ground—which is why I love salads so much. Salads are not only a celebration of whole foods, when beautiful greens remain in their most pure and freshest state but they're also an easy way to get your daily quota of vitamins and minerals—jazzed up with a well-balanced, zingy dressing. But there's nothing I hate more than eating a healthy salad for lunch, only to be left starving an hour later (which inevitably leads to a sabotaging sugar-hit at 3pm). This is when you suffer from salad fatigue, when all your good intentions backfire.

I understand why many people don't enjoy eating salad. With limp salad leaves, dry, discolored old vegetables, no dressing or even too much dressing, salad can be downright awful. Even more so than other dishes, a great salad is only as good as the quality of its ingredients. I love big, tasty salads that are balanced with the right amount of carbohydrate, vegetable, good fats and protein—which sustain your energy levels. Mother Nature does all the hard work so all you have to do is buy vegetables and fruits that are in season and think about creating texture (think crunchy cos leaves, a handful of nuts) and, if you're not a confident cook, work with classic flavor combinations like tomato and basil, smoked salmon and lemon, figs and prosciutto... the list is endless. I crave bowlfuls of the Beetroot-Stained Quinoa with Homemade Ricotta (pg 136) and the Crunchy Cauliflower and Almond Salad (pg 140) is a firm favorite amongst my friends.

CHILI AND GARLIC LABNEH SALAD
with watermelon and mint

Salty, sweet and super refreshing, this salad screams of summer. You can make your own labneh (strained yogurt cheese) or you can buy a good quality jar from your gourmet grocer. Fetta is saltier than labneh but also works well.

INGREDIENTS

125 g (4 oz) Chili and Garlic Labneh (pg 182) or
    store-bought (can substitute fetta)
1 kg (2 lb) watermelon flesh, thinly sliced, rind
    removed and cut into rough triangles
1 bunch fresh mint leaves, torn into pieces

Dressing

1 tablespoon extra virgin olive oil
1 tablespoon fresh lemon juice
sea salt

METHOD

1. Arrange watermelon on a platter and scatter with labneh and mint.
2. Whisk together the oil, lemon juice and salt. Drizzle dressing over salad and serve immediately.

I love serving this with an oily piece of pan-fried fish such as ocean trout or swordfish.

RIBBONED ASPARAGUS SALAD
with egg and fried capers

A classic egg and mayonnaise salad gets an upgrade with these crispy, nutty and fried capers. I urge you to try and make the whole egg mayonnaise from scratch—homemade mayonnaise will always have a more complex flavor and a fuller bodied texture than any store-bought variety.

INGREDIENTS

8 free-range eggs, room temperature

12 asparagus stalks, rinsed, woody ends removed and tips trimmed

4 tablespoons baby capers, drained

2 tablespoons extra virgin olive oil

4 scallions (spring onions), white part only, thinly sliced

2 tablespoons dill, roughly chopped

4 tablespoons (125 g/4 oz) Whole Egg Mayonnaise (pg 181)

2 tablespoons lemon juice

60 g (2 oz) baby rocket (arugula) leaves

sea salt and freshly ground pepper

METHOD

1. Bring a saucepan of water with a generous pinch of salt to the boil. Gently submerge eggs and cook for 7–8 minutes. Drain and run under cold water. Peel, discard shell and roughly chop. If you find peeling eggs a bit fiddly, peel them under cold running water—it helps remove the shell more easily.

2. Meanwhile, prepare the asparagus ribbons. Using a vegetable peeler, starting from the top of the spear, gently shave downward, to create a thin ribbon. Continue until you only have a small piece of the spear left, then run a small knife down the middle to separate. Slice all of the tips in half lengthwise. Don't worry about each ribbon being perfect; it's meant to be rustic. Set aside.

3. Using absorbent paper, pat the drained capers dry. In a small saucepan, heat the oil to medium-high. Add the baby capers. Cook for 1 minute stirring occasionally or until lightly golden. Use a slotted spoon to transfer to absorbent paper and set aside.

4. In a large bowl, combine chopped eggs, asparagus, scallions, dill, mayonnaise, lemon juice and rocket. Mix well and season to taste.

5. Divide salad between bowls, scatter with fried capers and serve.

GINGER POACHED CHICKEN SALAD
with sesame dressing

The magic of this recipe is truly in its simplicity. The salad builds on a base of finely shredded Chinese cabbage, tossed with cucumber, carrot, toasted almonds and poached chicken and drizzled with a full-bodied sesame dressing. If you're short on time, you can use barbecue chicken, rather than poaching the breast. Sesame paste can be found at Asian grocers however you can easily just substitute with tahini.

INGREDIENTS

Salad
750 g (1 lb 8 oz) free-range chicken breast fillets
6 cm (2½ inch) fresh ginger, sliced
1 Lebanese cucumber
1 carrot, peeled
2 tablespoons flaked almonds
300 g (10 oz) Chinese cabbage (wombok), finely
    shredded
2 scallions (spring onions), thinly sliced
1 large red chili, deseeded and thinly sliced
½ bunch cilantro (coriander) leaves

Sesame dressing
2 tablespoons sesame paste (or tahini)
2 tablespoons honey
3 tablespoons rice wine vinegar
3 tablespoons olive oil
2 tablespoons tamari
½ teaspoon sesame oil
sea salt and freshly ground black pepper, to taste

METHOD

1. Start by poaching the chicken. Place breast fillets in a saucepan with ginger and enough water to cover. Bring to the boil, then cover and reduce heat to low. Simmer until chicken is just cooked through, about 8–10 minutes. Remove and set aside to cool slightly. When cool enough to handle, shred chicken using your fingers.
2. Meanwhile, cut cucumber in half lengthwise and discard seeds using a spoon. Slice thinly, on the diagonal. Using a vegetable peeler, slice peeled carrot lengthways into long strips or ribbons.
3. Dry roast almonds over low-medium heat until lightly golden, stirring often. Set aside until ready to serve.
4. In a large bowl, combine cucumber, carrot ribbons, cabbage, scallions, chili, coriander and shredded chicken.
5. Whisk all sesame dressing ingredients in a bowl to combine. Taste and season with salt and pepper.
6. Before serving, toss salad with sesame dressing. Scatter with toasted almond flakes and serve in individual bowls.

EGGPLANT, FREEKEH AND PISTACHIO SALAD

with sumac vinaigrette

A good dressing is the soul of a salad—and this punchy combination of garlic, chili, sumac and red wine vinegar is no exception. Freekeh is wheat, but it's wheat that has been harvested when it's still young and green, and then it gets roasted. It's similar to barley in texture and flavor, but it has a slight smokiness. Pomegranate seeds are a wonderful addition but are not essential.

INGREDIENTS

Freekeh salad

1 large eggplant (aubergine), about 400 g (14 oz), cut into 1 cm (½ inch) cubes
3 tablespoons olive oil
½ medium Spanish onion, peeled and diced
1 garlic clove, peeled and finely chopped
200 g (7 oz) freekeh, washed and drained
150 ml (5 fl oz) good quality chicken stock
90 ml (3 oz) water
240 g tinned brown lentils
½ bunch cilantro (coriander), roughly chopped
½ bunch flat-leaf parsley, roughly chopped
½ bunch mint leaves, chopped

60 g (2 oz) pistachios, roughly chopped
sea salt and freshly ground black pepper
½ pomegranate, seeds removed (optional)

Dressing

4 tablespoons extra virgin olive oil
3 tablespoons red wine vinegar
2 garlic cloves, peeled and grated on a microplane
1 long red chili, thinly sliced
2 tablespoons lemon juice
3 teaspoons ground cumin
3 teaspoons sumac

METHOD

1. Preheat oven to 200°C (400°F).
2. To roast the eggplant, spread cubes out on baking tray and drizzle with 2 tablespoons of the olive oil. Cook for 25–30 minutes or until eggplant is tender and lightly golden. Set aside to cool.
3. Heat the remaining 1 tablespoon olive oil in a saucepan to medium-high. Add the onion and garlic and sauté until golden, about 3 minutes. Stir through washed freekeh, chicken stock and water. Cover and simmer for 15 minutes or until freekeh is tender and liquid has been absorbed. Set aside to cool.
4. Rinse lentils thoroughly under cold running water. Drain well and set aside.
5. Meanwhile, prepare the salad dressing. In a small bowl, whisk to combine all ingredients.
6. In a large serving bowl, combine roasted eggplant, freekeh, lentils, coriander, parsley, mint and pistachios. Add dressing and toss to combine. Season to taste. Scatter with pomegranate seeds (if using) and serve.

PARMESAN KALE SALAD

with pine nuts, pepitas and a runny poached egg

Kale, the divisive green, really is a superfood, full of iron, vitamin A, vitamin C and beta carotene. There's no denying it, raw kale can be tough and bitter but, if prepared properly, it can be a revelation. To me, this salad is the perfect dish to woo any anti-kalers—it truly is a game-changer. Pecorino, a hard cheese made from sheep's milk, has a sharper taste than Parmesan which works beautifully in this salad.

INGREDIENTS

Salad
1 bunch curly kale, about 200 g (7 oz), washed and dried
2 tablespoons pepitas
2 tablespoons pine nuts
3 tablespoons fresh Parmesan (or pecorino), finely grated on a microplane
1 lemon, cut into small wedges

Dressing
3 tablespoons extra virgin olive oil
1 tablespoon Whole Egg Mayonnaise (pg 181) or any good quality mayonnaise
1 lemon, juiced
1 teaspoon lemon zest
1 small garlic clove, peeled and finely grated on a microplane
salt and freshly ground pepper

Poached eggs
4 free-range eggs, room temperature
2 teaspoons apple cider vinegar

METHOD

1. Use a sharp knife to cut out the ribs of the kale leaves. Then, roll the de-ribbed leaves into a tight cigar shape and thinly slice into ribbons. Transfer the kale to a medium-sized serving bowl.
2. In a small non-stick frying pan, over a low heat dry roast pepitas and pine nuts until lightly golden, stirring constantly, about 1 minute.
3. In a small bowl, whisk to combine olive oil, mayonnaise, lemon juice, zest, garlic, salt and pepper.
4. Add the dressing to the kale. Using your hands, gently massage the dressing to coat all the leaves. This is the key to preparing kale— take time to massage the leaves as this softens them. If you can leave the salad for 20 minutes at this point, the dressing will tenderize the kale. Add Parmesan, pepitas and pine nuts and toss to combine.
5. To poach eggs, bring a medium saucepan of water to a simmer. Add vinegar and then carefully crack 1 egg into the water. Gently simmer for 3–4 minutes or until whites have firmed. Make sure the water does not boil. Remove egg with a slotted spoon and drain on absorbent paper. Repeat process with remaining eggs.
6. Divide kale between bowls and serve with a poached egg on top. Grate a little extra Parmesan on top and serve with a lemon wedge.

HERBED COUSCOUS
with roasted baby carrots and cranberries

Slow-roasting baby carrots brings out their natural sweetness and turns them into the hero of the dish. If you can get your hands on a bunch of heirloom carrots, this dish looks spectacular. Serve with the Slow Roasted Lamb Shoulder (pg 87) or Baked Side of Salmon with Tahini Yogurt and Herb Crust (pg 72) for a Sunday lunch. (It also manages to find its way onto our Christmas Day spread every year).

INGREDIENTS

18 heirloom or Dutch (baby) carrots, trimmed and
  scrubbed (reserve greenest leaves)
1 tablespoon extra virgin olive oil
200 g (7 oz) couscous
150 g (5 oz) Danish fetta, crumbled
3 tablespoons dried cranberries, roughly chopped
3 tablespoons pine nuts, toasted

Herb dressing
1 lemon, juiced
2 tablespoons olive oil
1 teaspoon ground cumin
1 teaspoon ground coriander
½ bunch cilantro (coriander), roughly chopped
½ bunch flat-leaf parsley, roughly chopped
handful of reserved carrot tops, roughly chopped
sea salt and freshly ground pepper

METHOD

1. Preheat oven to 200°C (400°F).
2. Place carrots on a roasting tray lined with baking (parchment) paper. Drizzle with oil and season with salt and pepper. Place in the oven for 20 minutes, turning occasionally and cook until carrots are caramelized and tender. Set aside to cool slightly.
3. Meanwhile, place couscous in a heatproof bowl. Stir in 400 ml (13 fl oz) boiling water until combined. Cover with plastic wrap and stand for 5 minutes, then fluff with a fork.
4. To make the dressing, combine the lemon juice, olive oil, ground cumin, ground coriander, herbs and carrot tops in a bowl. Whisk and season to taste.
5. In a large bowl, combine cooled carrots, couscous, fetta and cranberries. Add dressing and toss to combine. Divide between 4 bowls, scatter with pine nuts and drizzle with a little extra virgin olive oil.

If you're intolerant to wheat, use quinoa instead of couscous.

CHARRED CORN SALAD
with honey mustard dressing

Charring the corn gives this vibrant salad a smoky finish. Tossed through with a handful of cherry tomatoes, slithers of chili and a tangy-sweet honey dressing, this salad works a treat alongside the Jamaican Jerk Chicken or any barbecued dishes.

INGREDIENTS

1 tablespoon olive oil
2 x 150 g (5 oz) ears of corn
sea salt and freshly ground pepper
½ small Spanish onion, peeled and thinly sliced
  lengthways
1 avocado, halved, de-stoned and cut into cubes or
  slices
1 long red chili, seeds removed, thinly sliced
  lengthways
150 g (5 oz) baby cos lettuce, roughly torn

60 g (2 oz) cherry tomatoes, quartered
½ bunch cilantro (coriander), roughly chopped

Honey mustard dressing
2 tablespoons extra virgin olive oil
2 tablespoons apple cider vinegar
1 tablespoon honey
1 tablespoon Dijon mustard
1 garlic clove, peeled and grated on a microplane
¼ teaspoon sea salt

METHOD

1. Remove the outer husk from the corn and peel away the silk (white string).
2. Heat a hot grill or barbecue to medium-high. Pour oil over the corn and place directly on the heat.
3. Cook for 6–10 minutes, turning every few minutes, until evenly charred. Allow to cool and then stand each ear upright on its base and use a sharp knife to shave off the charred kernels.
4. To make the dressing, whisk together the olive oil, vinegar, honey, mustard, garlic and salt until emulsified. Toss to coat salad ingredients and pour over the corn. Mix thoroughly.
5. Serve with Jamaican Jerk Chicken (pg 97) or any barbecued dishes.

ROASTED BROCCOLI AND BRUSSELS SPROUT SALAD

with maple tahini dressing

Kale takes a supporting role in this sweet, tangy, creamy and completely addictive roasted broccoli and Brussels sprout salad. On paper, it looks like a relatively simple, uninspired salad but after you roast the broccoli and Brussels sprouts until they're crunchy and earthy and then toss them through this maple, tamari and tahini dressing, this is a winning dish.

INGREDIENTS

250 g (9 oz) broccoli florets, trimmed and cut into bite size pieces
150 g (5 oz) Brussels sprouts, trimmed, halved lengthways
2 tablespoons extra virgin olive oil
1 bunch curly kale, about 200 g (7 oz), washed and dried
1 avocado, diced

Maple tahini dressing
2 tablespoons tahini paste
1 teaspoon Dijon mustard
1 garlic clove, peeled and finely grated or crushed
2 tablespoons apple cider vinegar
1 tablespoon tamari sauce
2 tablespoons pure maple syrup
1 tablespoon extra virgin olive oil
sea salt and freshly ground pepper

METHOD

1. Preheat oven to 180°C (350°F).
2. Toss broccoli and Brussels sprouts with olive oil. Spread onto a lined baking tray and roast for 25–30 minutes or until golden around the edges and tender. Set aside to cool.
3. Meanwhile, use a sharp knife to cut out the ribs of the kale leaves. Then, roll the de-ribbed leaves into a tight cigar shape and thinly slice into ribbons. Transfer the kale to a medium serving bowl.
4. In a small mixing bowl, whisk together all the dressing ingredients. Some brands of tahini are thicker than others, so if your dressing is too thick, add a bit more water and/or vinegar to taste.
5. Pour the maple tahini dressing over the kale. Use your hands to massage the dressing through the leaves. This is the key to preparing kale—take time to massage the leaves as this softens them. Add cooled roasted broccoli and Brussels sprouts and lightly toss through. Taste and season accordingly. Scatter with sesame seeds and serve.

CUCUMBER, AVOCADO, MINT AND WATERCRESS SALAD

with lime sweet-and-sour dressing

The elements of this simple Asian-inspired salad are a match made in heaven. Ribbons of cooling cucumber, peppery watercress, picked ginger and avocado, tossed with a zingy lime, sweet-and-sour dressing, make this salad a crowd pleaser. If watercress is unavailable, substitute with rocket.

INGREDIENTS

4 small Lebanese cucumbers
1 avocado, diced
1 bunch of watercress, washed and broken into sprigs
½ bunch cilantro (coriander) leaves
½ bunch mint leaves
1 long fresh red chili, deseeded and thinly sliced
1 tablespoon pickled ginger, roughly chopped
   (optional)

Dressing

2 tablespoons lime juice (or lemon juice), freshly
   squeezed
2 tablespoons rice vinegar
2 teaspoons sugar
1 tablespoon gluten free fish sauce

METHOD

1. Make cucumber ribbons by running a vegetable peeler down the length of a cucumber stopping when you get to the seeds. Rotate the cucumber and do the same on the other side. Discard the middle section and repeat with the remaining cucumbers. Place cucumber ribbons, avocado, watercress, cilantro, mint, chili and pickled ginger (if using) in a large serving bowl. Mix gently and transfer to the refrigerator until ready to use.
2. For the lime dressing, place all ingredients in a bowl and whisk together until the sugar has dissolved.
3. Dress salad at the last minute tossing to ensure all the ingredients are combined. Serve with Tea-smoked Salmon (pg 43), Jamaican Jerk Chicken (pg 97) or Blackened Salmon (pg 80).

BEETROOT-STAINED QUINOA

with homemade ricotta and beet green chips

This beetroot-stained quinoa is insanely good. I hate throwing away any part of a vegetable—I eat the cores of every apple and pear—and in this recipe, I've included roasted beetroot leaves. If you can't buy beetroot with the greens still attached at your local grocer, you can use kale instead—just cut out the middle ribs and roast for 10 minutes.

INGREDIENTS

5 fresh baby beetroots, about 500 g (1 lb), leaves attached
200 g (7 oz) white quinoa, rinsed and drained
500 ml (16 fl oz) gluten free good quality vegetable or chicken stock (or water)
100 g (3½ oz) frozen peas (or snow peas)
3 tablespoons extra virgin olive oil

3 tablespoons lemon juice
2 tablespoons red wine vinegar
2 scallions (spring onions), thinly sliced
125 g (4 oz) Homemade Ricotta (pg 183) or store-bought
1 tablespoon pomegranate molasses (optional)
baby beetroot shoots (optional)

METHOD

1. Preheat oven to 200°C (400°F).
2. Remove beetroot leaves and set aside. Wrap each beetroot bulb in foil. Spread out on a baking tray and cook for 45–50 minutes or until tender. Check by piercing the beetroot with a skewer—there is no resistance when cooked.
3. While the beetroot is cooking, steam the quinoa. In a small saucepan, combine the quinoa and stock. Bring to the boil and cover. Reduce the heat and cook until the liquid has been absorbed and the quinoa is tender, about 15 minutes. Uncover, fluff with a fork and set aside.
4. With the reserved beet leaves, thoroughly wash in cold water then drain. Place in a bowl and toss with 1 tablespoon olive oil, making sure the leaves are evenly coated (you can use olive oil spray). Spread the beet greens in a single layer on a lined baking tray. Bake in the oven for 10 minutes or until greens are crisp. Sprinkle with salt and pepper and set aside.
5. Bring a small saucepan of salted water to the boil. Blanch peas for 2 minutes or until just cooked. Drain and set aside.
6. Once beetroot is cooked and is cool enough to handle, use plastic gloves to peel the beetroot. Cut beetroot in half, thinly slice and place in a medium bowl. Add remaining olive oil (2 tablespoons), lemon juice and red wine vinegar. Add the cooked quinoa and gently toss to combine.Stir through the peas, scallions and ricotta. Crush half the beet leaf chips and stir through. Drizzle with pomegranate molasses (if desired), scatter with remaining beet chips and baby beetroot shoots (if using).

RED QUINOA, SWEET POTATO AND GOAT'S CHEESE SALAD

This vibrantly-colored roast sweet potato and goat's cheese salad will redeem every lacklustre quinoa dish you've ever suffered through. It hits every salty, sweet, creamy, fresh and tangy note. You can roast pumpkin (squash) instead of the sweet potato.

INGREDIENTS

500 g (1 lb) sweet potato, peeled, cut into 2.5 cm (1 inch) cubes
2 tablespoons olive oil
180 g (6 oz) red quinoa, rinsed and drained
500 ml (16 fl oz) gluten free chicken stock
2 tablespoons sunflower seeds
2 tablespoons pine nuts

½ bunch mint, roughly chopped
½ bunch cilantro (coriander), roughly chopped
180 g (6 oz) goat's cheese, crumbled (or fetta)

Dressing
60 ml (2 fl oz) lemon juice
60 ml (2 fl oz) extra virgin olive oil

METHOD

1. Preheat oven to 200°C (400°F).
2. Toss sweet potato in a bowl with olive oil to coat. Spread evenly on tray and roast for 20–25 minutes or until lightly golden.
3. Meanwhile, place quinoa and stock in a saucepan over high heat. Bring to the boil and then cover. Reduce heat to a simmer and cook until the liquid has been absorbed and the quinoa is tender, about 15–18 minutes. Uncover, fluff the quinoa with a fork and set aside.
4. Heat a splash of oil in a non-stick frying pan and lightly sauté sunflower seeds and pine nuts until light golden. (Be careful, pine nuts cook more quickly than the sunflower seeds).
5. To make the dressing, whisk to combine lemon juice and extra virgin olive oil in a small bowl. Season with salt and pepper.
6. In a bowl, combine cooled quinoa, roasted sweet potato, sunflower seeds, pine nuts, herbs and goat's cheese.
7. Pour the dressing over salad and toss to combine. Divide salad evenly between bowls and serve.

CRUNCHY CAULIFLOWER, QUINOA AND ALMOND SALAD

This is a virtuous, hearty salad where cauliflower is the star. Along with Brussels sprouts and broccoli, cauliflower is a cruciferous vegetable that crisps up when frying and roasting. Here, we shallow-fry the cauliflower however you can also deep-fry it to give the salad a more intense flavor. Pomegranate molasses is available from select supermarkets and gourmet delicatessens.

INGREDIENTS

180 g (6 oz) tricolor quinoa (or white, red or black), rinsed and drained

500 ml (16 fl oz) gluten free chicken or vegetable stock (or water)

90 ml (3 fl oz) rice bran oil (or any neutral oil)

1 large cauliflower head, about 1 kg (2 lb), broken into small florets

½ bunch flat-leaf parsley, roughly chopped

½ bunch mint leaves, roughly chopped

6 scallions (spring onions), thinly sliced

sea salt and freshly ground black pepper

3 tablespoons whole almonds, roughly chopped

½ pomegranate, seeds (optional)

2 tablespoons pomegranate molasses (optional)

Sesame yogurt dressing

2 tablespoons tahini paste

2 garlic cloves, peeled and crushed

150 g (5 oz) gluten free Greek yogurt

1 lemon, juiced

2 teaspoons ground cumin

1 teaspoon ground coriander

1 teaspoon sumac*

METHOD

1. In a small saucepan, combine the quinoa and stock. Bring to the boil and cover. Reduce the heat and cook until the liquid has been absorbed and the quinoa is tender, about 15 minutes. Uncover, fluff quinoa with a fork. Transfer to a large bowl.
2. Meanwhile, to cook the cauliflower, add half the oil to a heavy-based saucepan over medium-high heat. In batches, cook the cauliflower florets, adding a little more oil with each batch, making sure not to overcrowd the pan. Cook for 6–10 minutes, turning so they are golden-brown all over. Transfer to a plate with absorbent paper and sprinkle with a little salt. Repeat with remaining cauliflower. You may need to add more oil so that all the cauliflower is golden and crunchy.
3. For the sesame yogurt dressing, combine all the ingredients in a bowl and whisk to combine.
4. To serve, combine the crunchy cauliflower, cooked quinoa, parsley, mint, scallions and sesame yogurt dressing in a bowl. Toss to make sure the dressing coats all the ingredients. Scatter with toasted almonds, pomegranate seeds and drizzle with pomegranate molasses. Serve in individual bowls.

To remove pomegranate seeds, slice the pomegranate in half horizontally. Hold one half with cut side down over a bowl. Spread your fingers slightly. Use a rolling pin or wooden spoon to tap (more of a whack) the top. The seeds will slip through your fingers into the bowl.

TO THE SIDE

Like my mother and grandmothers before me (and no doubt their mothers), the cook in me always wants to be sure there is enough food on the table. Heaven forbid, there won't be enough. That's why no matter how simple I plan dinner to be, our table ends up with a little bowl of yogurt dip, a jar of chutney, perhaps a fried egg, some steamed vegetables or, more often than not, one of the following side dishes.

The Stir-fried Green Beans with Honey and Miso (pg 144) are absolutely delicious and great served as part of an Asian-inspired banquet, together with Teriyaki Salmon (pg 52) and Sweet Spiced Duck Marylands with Chili and Plums (pg 100). Christmas wouldn't feel right without the Maple Roasted Root Vegetables with Green Sauce (pg 147) served alongside Slow Roasted Lamb Shoulder (pg 87). My husband is obsessed with the Chili and Fennel Sweet Potato Wedges (pg 145), requesting them as a side with almost every meal.

For me, there's something so nice about having a complimentary dish or two, to tie a meal together.

STIR FRIED GREEN BEANS
with honey and miso

This is, hands down, the best way to eat green beans. Since this dish screams of healthiness—as an elegant bundle of vitamin-rich greens—you can afford to coddle it, guilt-free, with honey and lots of oil. This is lovely served as part of an Asian-inspired banquet or as a side to Teriyaki Salmon with Fried Egg and Forbidden Rice (pg 52).

INGREDIENTS
60 ml (2 fl oz) rice bran oil
400 g (14 oz) green beans, topped and tailed
2 tablespoons white (shiro) miso paste
1 tablespoon honey
2 teaspoons tamari
1 teaspoon sesame oil
2 garlic cloves, peeled and roughly diced
1 long red chili, deseeded, halved and thinly sliced
2 teaspoons white sesame seeds

METHOD
1. Heat rice bran oil in a wok to high. Add beans, in batches, and cook until tender and the edges of the beans start to become golden, about 5–6 minutes. Remove with a slotted spoon, set aside on absorbent paper and repeat with remaining beans. Carefully discard excess hot oil from the wok, leaving about 1 teaspoon in the wok.
2. In a small bowl, whisk to combine the miso, honey, tamari and sesame oil.
3. Using the same wok, sauté the garlic and chili on medium-high heat until lightly golden. Return beans to wok and stir through the miso paste and honey mixture. Cook, stirring constantly, until beans are coated. Add sesame seeds and toss to combine. Serve immediately.

CHILI AND FENNEL SWEET POTATO WEDGES

with avocado and yogurt dip

Not only do sweet potatoes have a host of health benefits—with a low glycemic index and as an excellent source of vitamin A, vitamin C, potassium, iron—they're also inexpensive and, most importantly, taste absolutely delicious. The avocado and yogurt dip (which should really be called a whip because it's super thick) is a great accompaniment to balance out the spice from the sweet potato.

INGREDIENTS

Sweet potato wedges

800 g (1 lb 10 oz) sweet potato (orange or purple), unpeeled
2 tablespoons extra virgin olive oil
1 teaspoon fennel seeds, lightly crushed
1 teaspoon sea salt
¼ teaspoon dried chili flakes
¼ teaspoon freshly ground black pepper

Avocado and yogurt dip

1 ripe avocado, halved, seed removed and flesh scooped out
60 g (2 oz) gluten free Greek yogurt
1 garlic clove, peeled and finely grated on a microplane
1 tablespoon lemon juice
1 tablespoon fresh cilantro (coriander), finely chopped

METHOD

1. Preheat oven to 200°C.
2. Cut sweet potatoes into even sized wedges. Toss in olive oil and sprinkle with fennel seeds, salt, chili and pepper. Place sweet potatoes on a lined baking tray, in a single layer and roast for 30–40 minutes or until golden and crunchy.
3. While the sweet potatoes are roasting, place the avocado, Greek yogurt, garlic, lemon juice and cilantro in a food processor. Blend until smooth.
4. Serve avocado dip in a bowl alongside sweet potato wedges.

MAPLE ROASTED ROOT VEGETABLES
with green sauce

Roasting is a great way to cheer up any older vegetable that may have been left in the refrigerator too long. The vegetables all cook at different rates—so some are crunchier than others—which really is the beauty of this dish. The green chili and herb sauce balances out the sweetness of the maple spiced veggies and gives the dish a fresh lift.

INGREDIENTS

200 g (7 oz) parsnips, peeled and halved lengthways
300 g (10 oz) heirloom or Dutch (baby) carrots, trimmed
1 Spanish onion, peeled and cut into wedges
8 baby beetroots, trimmed, peeled and halved (mix of golden, red and yellow)
1 garlic clove, peeled and crushed
3 tablespoons pure maple syrup
60 ml (2 fl oz) extra virgin olive oil
sea salt and freshly ground pepper

Green sauce
1 green chili, deseeded and roughly chopped
2 cloves garlic, peeled and finely chopped
2 anchovy fillets, drained
1 bunch flat-leaf parsley leaves, roughly chopped
1 bunch mint leaves, roughly chopped
3 tablespoons extra virgin olive oil
1 tablespoon lemon juice
½ teaspoon sea salt

METHOD

1. Preheat oven to 200°C (400°F).
2. Start by prepping your vegetables. Cut into roughly even sized pieces. Place on a lined baking tray (or two), spreading in a single layer, making sure they're not over crowded.
3. Whisk to combine garlic, maple syrup, oil, salt and pepper in a bowl. Drizzle over vegetables. Use your hands to mix all the ingredients together to ensure all the root vegetables are coated. Roast for 45–50 minutes, tossing every 15 minutes or until golden and tender.
4. Meanwhile, to make the green sauce, place all the ingredients in a food processor and blend to form a smooth sauce of thick pouring consistency.
5. Place root vegetables on a platter and drizzle with green sauce.

SPICED PUMPKIN AND SPANISH ONION

with harissa yogurt

This roasted pumpkin dish is pimped up by a generous coating of sweet spices and a tangy Harissa yogurt. Cinnamon and cumin accentuate the natural sweetness of roasted pumpkin and onions, while fennel seeds have a liquorice taste which adds another layer of complexity. Harissa is a North African chili paste, available from most supermarkets, gourmet grocers and delicatessens.

INGREDIENTS

1.5 kg (3 lb) Japanese squash/pumpkin (kabocha) or butternut squash, de-seeded
3 Spanish onions, peeled

1 teaspoons chili flakes
1 teaspoons sea salt
½ teaspoons black pepper

Spice mix

3 tablespoons extra virgin olive oil
2 teaspoons cinnamon
2 teaspoons fennel seeds
2 teaspoons ground cumin
2 teaspoons cumin seeds

Harissa yogurt

280 g (9 oz) gluten free Greek yogurt
1 tablespoon lemon juice
1–2 teaspoons harissa paste, or more, if you like chili
6 sprigs cilantro (coriander)
30 g (1 oz) pine nuts, lightly toasted (optional)

METHOD

1. Preheat oven to 200°C (400°F).
2. Cut squash into thick wedges, leaving the skin on, to about 1 cm (½ inch) to 2 cm (¾ inch) at the thick end. Cut Spanish onion also into wedges, about 3 cm (1¼ inch) at the thick end.
3. In a large bowl, combine all the spice mix ingredients. Add squash and Spanish onion wedges and toss to combine. Spread, in a single layer, onto a baking tray (or two).
4. Roast for 40–45 minutes, turning the squash and Spanish onion occasionally. Keep an eye on the Spanish onion as it cooks faster than the pumpkin.
5. Meanwhile, combine the yogurt, lemon juice and harissa paste in a bowl.
6. Arrange the roasted vegetables on a serving platter. Drizzle with harissa yogurt and scatter with coriander and pine nuts (if using).

CRISP BRUSSELS SPROUTS
with spicy chipotle aioli

Don't like Brussels sprouts? Well, I'm about to turn your world upside down. Steamed, baked or fried – I'm obsessed with the good old sprout but these fellas, shallow-fried until they're charred and crunchy and then dipped in a smoky-spicy creamy chipotle aioli, you'll soon forget your Grandma's soggy boiled sprouts ever existed.

INGREDIENTS

500 g (1 lb) Brussels sprouts, rinsed and thoroughly dried
60 ml (2 fl oz) olive oil
1 teaspoon sea salt
½ teaspoon freshly ground black pepper

Spicy chipotle aioli
4 tablespoons Whole Egg Mayonnaise (pg 183)
2 teaspoons chipotle chili in adobo sauce
1 tablespoon lime juice
¼ teaspoon smoked paprika
1 teaspoon pure maple syrup

METHOD

1. Trim sprout stems and cut in half lengthways. If your sprouts are particularly large, you may want to cut them into quarters.
2. Heat a frying pan to medium-high and add the oil. Once the pan is hot, cook sprouts, in batches, turning occasionally until lightly golden all over. Remove with a slotted spoon and transfer to absorbent paper. Immediately sprinkle with salt and pepper. Repeat until all the Brussels sprouts are golden. You may need to add more oil, depending on the size of your frying pan.
3. Meanwhile, make the spicy chipotle aioli. Place all the ingredients in a food processor or blender. Process until smooth.
4. Serve crunchy sprouts hot with chipotle aioli on the side.

*Chipotle chilies in adobo are available from gourmet grocers however
you can substitute with Tabasco, Sriracha or any chili sauce.*

CUCUMBER AND CHILI RELISH

Side dishes can often bring together an entire meal. I would rarely serve my Cheeky Chicken Satay Skewers without this versatile relish. The white vinegar dressing in this relish balances out the heavily-spiced skewers, adding a punchy crunchiness to the dish.

INGREDIENTS

60 ml (2 fl oz) white vinegar
60 ml (2 fl oz) water
2 tablespoons white sugar
¼ teaspoon salt
1 small Lebanese cucumber, finely diced
1 long red chili, de-seeded and thinly sliced
½ bunch cilantro (coriander), roughly chopped

METHOD

1. Heat vinegar, water, sugar and salt in a small saucepan. Bring to the boil, stirring to ensure all the sugar has dissolved.
2. Allow to cool. In a medium bowl, combine the chopped cucumber and chili.
3. Stir through dressing and add cilantro just before serving.
4. Serve with Cheeky Chicken Satay (pg 55), Beef Rendang (pg 61) or as a part of any Asian-inspired banquet.

SWEET LITTLE THINGS

My love of cooking began with Saturday morning baking sessions; Mum would sit me on our apple green bench top. I'd stir the cake mix while she sifted, measured and did all the important jobs. Every time Mum turned her back, I'd lick the spoon. I always thought I was so secretive but, apparently Mum knew all about it.

From apple tea cakes and fresh pikelets to date-studded scones, I have always adored baking. There are no fancy, tricky recipes here—these are the desserts cooked by women like my mum, granny and nanny. They needed to feed and fill our hungry growing tummies and bring joy to the day. These sweet treats use simple ingredients, mostly inspired by seasonal fruits, and require minimal kitchen equipment.

Use the recipes as inspiration to play around with whatever fruits are in season. The Raspberry and Apple Crumble (pg 158) will still be delicious if you swap strawberries for the raspberries or add ground macadamias instead of the almonds. Serve the Black Sticky Rice (pg 156) with fresh mango or drizzle butterscotch sauce over poached nectarines, instead of using pears.

The important thing about baking is to create dishes that work for you. Often recipes require obscure equipment or expensive ingredients—these dishes are simple, wholesome and, most importantly, a pleasure to make.

CINNAMON SPICED APPLE FRITTERS

Often the simplest recipes are the most impressive. These apple fritters are a knockout. The best way to eat this dish is without restraint: generously dusted with icing sugar and then dunked into a bowl of Butterscotch Sauce with a scoop of Vanilla Bean Ice-cream to the side.

INGREDIENTS
2 Granny Smith apples
50 g (2 oz) all purpose (plain) flour
½ teaspoon cinnamon
100 ml (3½ oz) soda water
50 g (2 oz) ice cubes
sunflower oil
icing sugar (optional)

METHOD
1. Peel and core apples and then cut into rings, about ½ cm (¼ inch) in width.
2. Using a fork, Add flour, cinnamon, soda water and ice to a bowl and roughly mix together with a fork.
3. Add sunflower oil to a deep-fryer or to a frying pan to a depth of 2 cm (¾ inch). When ready to cook (and eat), heat the oil to 170°C (325°F). If shallow frying, use a candy thermometer or drop a cube of bread into the oil. If it turns golden in about 30 seconds, it's ready. Any faster and it will be too hot.
4. Dip each apple ring into the batter and shake off excess liquid.
5. Lower each fritter very carefully into the hot oil. Fry in batches, for around 5 minutes, turning the fritters around in the oil from time to time until they are evenly golden brown and crisp. Use a slotted spoon to remove and drain on absorbent paper.
6. Sprinkle with icing sugar and add Butterscotch Sauce (pg 161) and Vanilla Bean Ice-cream (pg 177). Serve immediately.

BLACK STICKY RICE
with caramelized pineapple

I'm a coconut fiend and this sweet, nutty, creamy rice pudding hits the sweet spot. Black sticky rice, also known as black glutinous rice, is a long-grain, sweet rice variety that becomes sticky and glutinous when cooked. When mangoes are in season, I simply slice fresh pieces on top, instead of the pineapple.

INGREDIENTS

200 g (7 oz) black sticky rice
100 g (3½ oz) light palm sugar
sea salt
250 ml (8 fl oz) coconut cream

Caramelized pineapple
½ fresh sweet pineapple, peeled, core removed and
   cut into long, thin wedges
2 tablespoons brown sugar
1 tablespoon butter

METHOD

1. Rinse the rice under cold running water, stirring to remove any husks or impurities. Drain and place in a medium saucepan and cover with enough water to cover the rice by 2.5 cm (1 inch).
2. Bring to the boil and then reduce heat to low. Cook, uncovered stirring occasionally for 30 minutes. At this point, check if the rice is done—all the water should have been absorbed and the rice should be soft with a slight bite from the outer husk. Add the shaved palm sugar, salt and 180 ml (6 fl oz) coconut cream. Stir through and cook for a further 5 minutes. Once combined, set aside.
3. To cook the caramelized pineapple, sprinkle both sides of the pineapple with sugar. Melt the butter in a non-stick frying pan over high heat until foaming. Add pineapple pieces and cook for 2 minutes each side or until lightly golden. You can also use a grill to cook the pineapple. Toss the pieces in sugar and butter before and grill until lightly charred.
4. To serve, return the black sticky rice to a low heat and stir until heated through. Scoop sticky rice into individual serving dishes. Divide remaining coconut cream between each bowl. Top with caramelized pineapple and serve.

BALSAMIC FIGS
with spiced crème anglaise

Caramelized balsamic figs, served in a pool of spiced crème anglaise (also called stirred custard), is one of my favorite desserts. When selecting figs, try to pick the ones that are heavy, plump and almost look like they'll split at the bottom. Crème anglaise will keep in the refrigerator for about one week.

INGREDIENTS

Spiced crème anglaise
250 ml (8 fl oz) full cream milk
250 ml (8 fl oz) pouring cream
1 vanilla bean pod, split and seeds scraped (or 2
   teaspoons vanilla bean paste)
1 cinnamon stick
1 star anise
4 free-range egg yolks
75 g (2½ oz) superfine (caster) sugar

Caramelized figs
1 tablespoon butter
1 tablespoon light brown sugar
4 figs, halved lengthwise
2 teaspoons balsamic vinegar

METHOD

1. To make crème anglaise, combine milk, cream, vanilla bean, cinnamon and star anise in a saucepan over low heat and bring to a simmer. Remove from heat.
2. Meanwhile, whisk egg yolks and sugar in a bowl until thick and pale. Pour, whisking constantly, into the hot milk mixture. Return saucepan to heat and cook stirring constantly for 5–8 minutes or until thick enough to coat the back of a wooden spoon. Using a sieve, strain mixture into a jug or bowl placed over ice and cool.
3. To caramelize the figs, melt the butter in a large frying pan over medium-high heat. Sprinkle the sugar over the base of the pan and place the figs, cut-side down, on top of the sugar. Cook the figs for 1–2 minutes or until lightly golden. Turn the figs and cook for another minute or so. The cooking time will depend on how ripe the figs are.
4. Drizzle over balsamic vinegar and gently toss the figs to allow the vinegar to coat. Serve figs in a pool of crème anglaise.

RASPBERRY AND APPLE CRUMBLE BAKE

Crumble is one of the most humble desserts with its crunchy topping and par-cooked fruit, served with a dollop of double cream and ice-cream. Few dishes are more satisfying. Using frozen berries allows you to cook this recipe all year round however it works equally well with almost any fruit combination—apple and rhubarb, blueberry and raspberry, pear and cherry.

INGREDIENTS

Raspberry and apple
3 Granny Smith (green) apples, about 400 g (14 oz)
200 g (7 oz) frozen raspberries, thawed
1 tablespoon pure maple syrup
1 teaspoon ground cinnamon

Crumble
3 tablespoons pure maple syrup
1 tablespoon butter (or coconut oil)
½ teaspoon cinnamon
100 g (3½ oz) ground almond meal (or any other ground nuts)
90 g (3 oz) gluten free rolled oats
olive oil spray, to grease
double cream

METHOD

1. Preheat oven to 180°C (350°F).
2. Peel, core and quarter the apples and cut into even-sized small chunks. Place in a medium saucepan with raspberries, maple syrup and cinnamon. Add 4 tablespoons of boiling water. Cover and simmer for 10–15 minutes or until the fruit is cooked (but not so soft that it breaks up).
3. In a small saucepan, heat maple syrup, butter and cinnamon until melted. Place ground almonds and rolled oats in a bowl. Pour melted syrup mixture over and stir until the oats and almonds are coated.
4. Lightly spray a 24 cm (9½ inch) square baking dish with olive oil spray. Transfer softened apples and raspberries to baking dish and scatter crumble evenly on top. Bake for 25–30 minutes or until the crumble is golden. Serve with a generous dollop of double cream and Vanilla Bean Ice-cream (pg 177).

CIDER AND CARDAMOM POACHED PEARS

with butterscotch sauce

These pears absorb the aromatics of the cardamom and cinnamon beautifully in this dessert. Butterscotch is a simple combination of brown sugar and butter—a little nuttier and less sweet than caramel. If you don't have cider, you can substitute with red wine or even water, just add a little sugar.

INGREDIENTS

Poached pears

500 ml (16 fl oz) pear (or apple), cider
500 ml (16 fl oz) water
2 cardamom pods, whole
1 cinnamon stick
1 vanilla bean, split lengthways and seeds scraped
4 ripe but firm pears (I like Beurré Bosc), peeled and
    left whole
60 g (2 oz) flaked almonds

Butterscotch sauce

150 ml (5 fl oz) pure cream
90 g (3 oz) brown sugar
60 g (2 oz) unsalted butter, cubed
1 teaspoon vanilla extract

METHOD

1. To poach the pears, place the cider, water, cardamom, cinnamon stick and vanilla bean in a large saucepan. Bring to the boil, then reduce heat to a simmer and add the pears. (The pears should be ¾ submerged. Add more cider or water if necessary.) Cover and simmer for 20–25 minutes or until you can insert a knife into the pears without any resistance. Once cooked, allow pears to cool in the saucepan.
2. Meanwhile, make the butterscotch sauce. Place the cream, brown sugar, butter and vanilla in a heavy-based saucepan and stir over medium heat until all ingredients have combined. Increase heat to high and bring to the boil, then reduce to low and simmer, uncovered, stirring often until the sauce thickens slightly (about 5 minutes). Set aside.
3. In a non-stick frying pan, dry roast flaked almonds, shaking the pan every few minutes. Cook until lightly golden. Set aside.
4. To serve, place a pear in the bottom of the bowl and drizzle with butterscotch sauce. Sprinkle with toasted flaked almonds and serve with a scoop of Vanilla Bean Ice-cream (pg 177). The pears can be served warm, at room temperature or chilled.

AMANDA'S BITTER CHOCOLATE MOUSSE

with caramelized blood orange and rosemary

One of my best friends, Amanda, is a chocolatier so I'm very lucky to have a steady supply of her gorgeous, hand-made, organic chocolate. What I love about her chocolates is that they aren't sickly sweet and she uses aromatics and spices. This chocolate mousse is inspired by her. The quality of the chocolate you use is key to a good mousse – so buy the best quality you can afford.

INGREDIENTS

Chocolate mousse

250 ml (8 fl oz) pure cream
150 g (5 oz) good quality dark (bittersweet) chocolate, roughly chopped
3 free-range eggs, separated
30 g (1 oz) superfine (caster) sugar

Caramelized blood oranges

2 blood oranges100 g (3½ oz) superfine (caster) sugar
2 tablespoons water
Sprig of rosemary, broken into pieces (optional)

METHOD

1. Whisk cream in a bowl until soft peaks form. Set aside.
2. Melt chocolate in a heatproof bowl over a saucepan of gently simmering water, making sure the bottom of the bowl is not in contact with the water. Turn off heat and allow to cool. Add yolks to the chocolate and stir to combine. Add whipped cream and fold through. In a separate bowl, beat egg whites and sugar until soft peaks form. Add to the chocolate mixture and fold to combine. Divide between four serving bowls and place in the refrigerator to chill for 2 hours or preferably overnight.
3. Meanwhile, prepare the blood oranges. Remove the skins and pith from the oranges with a knife. Slice the oranges thinly into discs and place in a single layer in a shallow serving dish. Top with rosemary sprigs.
4. Place the sugar and water in a heavy-based saucepan over high heat. Cook, without stirring, until it forms a lightly golden caramel. Immediately remove from the heat and carefully drizzle over the blood oranges. It may spit and splutter at this point. Allow to cool before placing in the refrigerator for 2 hours (this allows the caramel to soften and turn into a sauce).
5. Arrange the oranges and syrup on top of the mousse and serve immediately.

Substitute with just plain old oranges, red navel oranges, mandarins or you can even use pink grapefruit (just add a little more sugar).

WARM APPLE PIE

There is nothing more satisfying than a slice of warm apple pie, served with a dollop of double cream and a scoop of ice-cream. The pastry for this apple pie is very short (which means it has a high butter content), so you have to work quickly so the butter doesn't melt from the warmth of your hands.

INGREDIENTS

Apple filling

6 large Granny Smith apples, about 1 kg (2 lb) after
    apples have been peeled and cored
180 g (6 oz) superfine (caster) sugar
2 tablespoons cold water
1 teaspoon cinnamon
¼ teaspoon ground cloves (optional)
½ small lemon zest
2 tablespoons unsalted butter
2 teaspoons English Breakfast marmalade

Pastry

150 g (5 oz) unsalted butter, chopped, room
    temperature
2 tablespoons boiling water
250 g (9 oz) self-rising (self-raising) flour, sifted
¼ teaspoon salt
melted butter
2–3 tablespoons milk
1 tablespoon superfine (caster) sugar
double cream

METHOD

1. Preheat oven to 180°C (350°F).
2. To make the filling, peel the apples. Halve, remove the core and cut into uneven pieces. You want the filling to have texture so cutting the apples into various sizes will mean some pieces will be softer than others.
3. Place the apple pieces, sugar, water, cinnamon, ground cloves (if using) and lemon zest in a large saucepan over medium heat. Cook stirring occasionally for 4 minutes or until sugar dissolves. Bring to the boil, then reduce heat to medium-low. Cover and cook stirring occasionally for 20 minutes or until apples are tender but retain their shape. Remove from the heat and strain most of the liquid (leaving about 3 tablespoons left in the saucepan). Stir in the butter and marmalade and set aside to cool completely.
4. For pastry, place butter and boiling water in a bowl. Using the back of a fork, mash to combine. Add sifted flour and salt and stir until it forms a soft dough. Shape into two flat, even discs. Wrap in plastic wrap and refrigerate for 30 minutes.
5. Once pastry has chilled, place one disc between two sheets of baking (parchment) paper and roll to a 25 cm (10 inch) circle that is large enough to fit in the base of your pie dish.
6. Lightly grease a round 21 cm (8¼ inch) x 3 cm (1¼ inch) deep pie dish with melted butter and line with one of the rolled pastries. Fill the dish with the cooled apple mixture.
7. Roll the remaining pastry between two sheets of baking (parchment) paper to a 23 cm (9 inch) circle for the pie lid. Gently lift the pastry lid on top of the apple mixture.
8. Trim the pastry to create a narrow rim around the dish, then press the edges together. You can use the back of a fork to crimp the edges.
9. Brush the pie top with milk and sprinkle with sugar. Bake for 30 minutes or until lightly golden.
10. Serve in bowls, with a generous dollop of double cream and Vanilla Bean Ice-cream (pg 177).

RICE PUDDING
with roasted peaches and cinnamon pepitas

A classic vanilla rice pudding gets an upgrade with peaches roasted in Pedro Ximenez (a dark, sweet Spanish sherry) and cinnamon-spiced pepitas. You can substitute plums or pears for the peaches. Pedro Ximénez is available from select bottle shops but sweet sherry is a good substitute.

INGREDIENTS

Rice pudding
150 g (5 oz) short-grain arborio rice
850 ml (1¾ pints) full cream milk
½ teaspoon vanilla extract
½ teaspoon ground cinnamon
¼ teaspoon sea salt
60 g (2 oz) superfine (caster) sugar
1 free-range egg yolk
30 g (1 oz) unsalted butter

Caramelized peaches
4 peaches
60 ml (2 fl oz) Pedro Ximenez sherry
1 tablespoon soft brown sugar
1 thin strip lemon zest, white pith removed
1 vanilla bean pod, split and seeds scraped

Spiced pepitas
100 g (3½ oz) pepitas (pumpkin seeds)
1 tablespoon pure icing sugar, sifted
1 teaspoon cinnamon

METHOD

1. Preheat oven to 200°C (400°F).
2. For the pudding, place the rice, milk, vanilla, cinnamon and salt in a large saucepan and bring to the boil. Reduce heat to low. Simmer uncovered, stirring occasionally, for 15–20 minutes or until rice is cooked but still has a slight bite (*al dente*). Add the sugar, stirring to dissolve. Remove from the heat, allow to cool slightly and then stir through the egg yolk and butter.
3. Divide the rice between serving bowls. Cover with cling wrap and place in the refrigerator to chill (if preferred) or set aside.
4. To prepare the roasted peaches, using a sharp knife, cut peaches in half and prize out the stone. Lay the peach halves, cut side up, in a roasting tray so they fit snugly. Drizzle the sherry over the peaches and sprinkle with brown sugar. Tuck in the lemon zest and vanilla bean. Cover with foil, sealing the tray and roast for 15 minutes. Remove the foil and cook for a further 15 minutes, uncovered – the peaches should be soft, slightly sticky and a caramel color. Allow to cool at room temperature.
5. For the pepitas, heat a frying pan to medium. Add the pepitas, sifted icing sugar and cinnamon. Cook, stirring and shaking the pan regularly, until lightly golden and caramelized. Remove from heat, set pepitas aside on a plate and allow to cool.
6. Top rice pudding with caramelized peaches and scatter with pepitas.

CHILLED OUT

I love ice-cream, sorbet, panna cotta, fro-yo (frozen yogurt), granita and gelato—anything chilled and creamy and I can't resist—which is why I had to include this chapter in the book. Most of the ice-cream recipes require an ice-cream maker however I have included my No-churn Caramelized Banana and Peanut Butter 'Ice-cream' (pg 172) for a manual option which is perfect for when you're craving a guilt-free sweet treat (you can even have it for breakfast the next morning, it's that healthy!) If you don't already have an ice-cream maker, once you get one, you won't waste time in the supermarket freezer aisle again. Try the Raspberry Swirl Frozen Yogurt (pg 170). It's the ultimate fro-yo, perfect to cool you down on sweltering summer days.

This chapter extends beyond our frozen friends with a dreamy Rhubarb and Pistachio Fool (pg 174) where layers of tart fruit and whipped cream create a not-too-sweet dessert. Coconut milk lightens the traditional all-cream panna cotta base in the Kaffir Lime and Lemongrass Pots (pg 173) without sacrificing lusciousness.

RASPBERRY SWIRL FROZEN YOGURT

A truly sensational dessert—it's creamy and luscious yet tart and refreshing. One scoop is never enough. The beauty of making your own frozen yogurt is that you can create your own combinations—so you can easily substitute with any fruit (mango and coconut swirl is a delicious personal favorite).

INGREDIENTS

Yogurt gelato
375 ml (12 fl oz) milk
150 g (5 oz) superfine (caster) sugar
125 g (4 oz) glucose syrup
500 g (1 lb) Greek yogurt

Raspberry coulis
125 g (4 oz) frozen raspberries, thawed (or fresh)
2 tablespoons superfine (caster) sugar

METHOD

1. At least 24 hours before you plan to churn the frozen yoghurt, place the ice-cream machine's bowl in the freezer (I have forgotten to do this so many times that I had to put it in as an instruction)
2. Combine the milk, sugar and glucose in a heavy based saucepan over medium heat and stir until the sugar has dissolved. Bring to the boil, take off the heat and then allow to cool completely.
3. Put the yogurt in a bowl and then whisk in cooled milk mixture until combined. Refrigerate until cold and then churn in an ice-cream machine according to the manufacturer's instructions.
4. Meanwhile, to make the raspberry coulis, place the raspberries and sugar in a small saucepan. Simmer for 5 minutes or until the sugar has dissolved and the coulis has thickened. I like texture so I tend to leave the raspberry seeds in, however, if you prefer a smoother consistency, push the coulis through a sieve and discard seeds. Allow to cool completely.
5. Place churned yogurt gelato into a 1.5 L (2½ pint) container and gently swirl the raspberry coulis through. If you like a soft-serve consistency, eat immediately. Otherwise cover with plastic wrap and freeze for 6 hours for a firmer texture.

COCONUT AND LIME SORBET WITH LYCHEES

This gelato recipe is almost fool-proof as there's no custard base (hence, no fear of curdling). Egg-free ice-creams often freeze rock solid so I suggest you eat this freshly churned or, if you do freeze it, allow to soften at room temperature before serving. This makes a quick, simple yet impressive dinner party dessert.

INGREDIENTS

2 x 400 ml (14 fl oz) tinned coconut cream
150 g (5 oz) superfine (caster) sugar
3 tablespoons lime juice
2 teaspoons lime zest
1 teaspoon salt
1 teaspoon vanilla extract
50 g (2 oz) desiccated coconut (can use shredded for
    a coarser texture)
fresh lychees, peeled, halved and pitted or tinned
    lychees, drained

METHOD

1. At least 24 hours before you plan to churn the sorbet, place the ice-cream machine's bowl in the freezer.
2. Pour the coconut cream, sugar, lime juice, zest, salt and vanilla into a medium saucepan. Cook, stirring occasionally, over medium-low heat until the sugar has dissolved. Transfer to a refrigerator for 2 hours or until completely cold.
3. Churn in an ice-cream machine according to manufacturer's instructions or until it reaches a soft-serve consistency.
4. Stir through desiccated coconut and serve immediately with fresh or tinned lychees or freeze for a firmer texture. If freezing, transfer to a container and press a piece of plastic wrap against the surface to prevent ice crystals from forming. After freezing, allow to soften at room temperature before serving.

NO-CHURN CARAMELIZED BANANA AND PEANUT BUTTER ICE-CREAM

I wasn't sure if this should go in breakfast or dessert because, quite honestly, it could go in both. The natural creamy texture of bananas gives this refined sugar free frozen treat a delightful consistency. I love sweet and salty desserts, which is why I've added the salt at the end but feel free to leave it out.

INGREDIENTS

4 medium ripe bananas, about 750 g (1 lb 8 oz),
   chopped into 2 cm (¾ inch) pieces
1 tablespoon butter (or coconut oil)
3 tablespoons crunchy peanut butter
1 tablespoon pure maple syrup
½ teaspoon vanilla
2 tablespoons dairy, soy or almond milk
½ teaspoon salt

METHOD

1. In a large frying pan, melt the butter over medium heat. Add the chopped bananas, flat side down, and caramelize for several minutes. Use a spatula to flip the bananas and caramelize on the other side. Remove from the heat and allow to cool slightly.
2. Place the caramelized bananas onto a tray lined with baking (parchment) paper. Make sure to scrape off all the delicious caramelized bits that are stuck to the pan. Place in the freezer for 2 hours or until completely frozen.
3. To make the 'ice-cream', place frozen banana in a blender with the peanut butter, maple syrup, vanilla and milk. Puree until smooth. Taste and season with salt, if necessary. Some peanut butters have a much higher salt content so adjust accordingly.
4. Serve immediately or transfer to the freezer for a firmer texture.

KAFFIR LIME AND LEMONGRASS POTS
infused coconut panna cotta

This lemongrass and kaffir lime panna cotta is so silky that it trembles and shakes when you jiggle it. Most fresh fruits will work well, especially pineapple and cherries. In winter, try poached pears or quinces.

INGREDIENTS

Panna cotta
2½ gelatine sheets
1 x 400 ml (13 fl oz) tinned coconut milk
250 ml (8 fl oz) pure cream
3 tablespoons light palm sugar, roughly chopped
6 kaffir lime leaves, crushed
1 stem lemon grass, white part only, roughly chopped

Mango salsa
1 ripe mango
1 teaspoon kaffir lime zest (or lime), grated on a microplane
1 teaspoon lime juice

METHOD
1. Place the gelatine sheets in a small bowl and cover with cold water. Set aside for 5 minutes to soften.
2. Combine the coconut milk, cream, palm sugar, kaffir lime leaves and lemon grass in a saucepan over medium heat. Stir for 5 minutes or until the palm sugar has dissolved. Remove from heat and set aside.
3. Remove gelatine from the water, squeezing out any excess liquid. Add gelatine to the coconut milk mixture and stir until it has dissolved. Set aside for 1 hour. Pour panna cotta mixture through a sieve and discard kaffir lime leaves and lemongrass. Divide mixture between four bowls and place in the refrigerator for at least 4 hours.
4. Meanwhile, to make the mango salsa, peel and dice mango into small, even chunks. Place in a small bowl and add zest and lime juice.
5. Top panna cotta with mango salsa and serve.

The type of gelatine you use is important. This recipe calls for the standard gelatine you can buy in supermarkets. However, titanium and gold strength varieties are also available. If using titanium or gold strength gelatine, read the packet instructions as the quantities and setting time will be different.

RHUBARB AND PISTACHIO FOOL

This classic British dessert is so simple yet impressive. Fools are traditionally made with just cream however I have added some Greek yogurt, to keep it light and fresh. Rhubarb has an unapologetic tartness that is a perfect match for this super-creamy dessert. You can cook this dish all year round by swapping the rhubarb for raspberries, strawberries and even apples and pears.

INGREDIENTS

60 g (2 oz) unsalted butter
100 g (3½ oz) soft brown sugar
500 g (1 lb) rhubarb, roughly chopped
1 vanilla bean pod, whole
300 ml (10 fl oz) double cream
125 g (4 oz) gluten free Greek yogurt
75 g (2½ oz) roasted pistachios, shelled and roughly
    chopped

METHOD

1. Combine butter and sugar in a saucepan over low heat, stirring until the sugar has dissolved. Add the rhubarb and vanilla bean pod and cook gently until tender, about 10–15 minutes. Remove vanilla bean pod and discard. Set aside to cool completely.
2. Using hand-held beaters or an electric mixer, whip the cream until soft peaks form, then stir in the yogurt.
3. Reserving a little of the syrup, fold the rest into the whipped cream and yogurt.
4. Divide between four bowls or serving glasses and drizzle over with the reserved rhubarb syrup. Scatter with chopped pistachios and serve.

Greek yogurt can be substituted with mascarpone if you're not using rhubarb, as it gives the dish a tangy acidity

VANILLA BEAN ICE-CREAM

Everyone should have a basic vanilla bean ice-cream recipe in their repertoire. This uses half milk and half cream, which creates a rich, silky ice-cream. You need to be patient when making the custard base as it can curdle quickly. This recipe can be used to make a range of ice-creams. Think crushed Oreos, salted caramel, Raspberry Coulis (pg 170), Butterscotch Sauce (pg 161). The possibilities are endless.

INGREDIENTS
500 ml (1 pint) pouring cream
500 ml (1 pint) full cream milk
1 vanilla bean pod, split lengthways (or ½ teaspoon
    vanilla bean paste)
pinch of salt
8 free-range egg yolks
500 g (1 lb) superfine (caster) sugar

METHOD
1. At least 24 hours before you plan to churn, place the ice-cream machine's bowl in the freezer.
2. Combine cream, milk, vanilla bean (seeds scraped) and salt in a saucepan over medium-high heat and bring to the boil. Set aside to cool slightly.
3. Meanwhile, using hand-held beaters or an electric mixer, whisk egg yolks with sugar until pale. Pour into the saucepan with the cream and milk, whisking. Return the saucepan to a low heat and cook. Stir constantly until the custard has thickened enough to coat the back of a wooden spoon. Strain through a fine sieve into a large bowl over ice. Cool to room temperature.
4. When cold, churn in an ice-cream machine according to manufacturer's instructions. Serve directly from the machine for soft serve, or store in freezer until needed.

PANTRY ESSENTIALS

These are the basic recipes that make up the backbone of many of the recipes in this book. Life doesn't always allow for homemade chicken stock but, when it does, gosh, it's good.

Homemade Ricotta (pg 183) and Labneh (pg 182) seem daunting to the uninitiated but I can't express how simple and easy they are—and the homemade variety is always tastier.

If you open my refrigerator on any day of the week, you'll always find a jar of Whole Egg Mayonnaise (pg 181) in the door ready to add to Ribboned Asparagus Salad with Egg and Fried Capers (pg 126) or to toss through a Parmesan Kale Salad (pg 131).

The four steamed rice recipes are the only recipes you'll ever need to suit every type of dish—from South East Asian curries and Japanese rice bowls to recipes inspired by the other sub-continental countries.

HOMEMADE CHICKEN STOCK

Mum is obsessed with making homemade chicken stock so I have included her recipe. It's dead easy, doesn't require tremendous amount of attention and really does make a world of difference in all kinds of dishes. You can freeze any leftover stock, which particularly comes in handy when making soups and risottos—both of which really benefit from using quality, homemade stock.

INGREDIENTS

1 kg (2 lb) free-range chicken necks
2 brown onions, skin on, roughly chopped
2 carrots, skin on, roughly chopped
1 leek, white part only, roughly chopped
2 celery sticks, including leaves, roughly chopped

2 fresh bay leaves
8 white peppercorns
1 sprig fresh thyme
2 sprigs flat-leaf parsley, roughly chopped

METHOD

1. In a large stockpot, combine all ingredients and fill with just enough water to cover.
2. Bring slowly to a simmer. When the stock just starts to bubble, skim off any froth from the top using a ladle. Reduce the heat to a gentle simmer and cook for 3 hours.
3. Pass through a large sieve and discard the chicken, vegetables and herbs. Allow stock to cool and remove any fat that has risen to the surface.
4. Store chicken stock in an airtight container. It will keep refrigerated for up to 3 days and frozen for up to 1 month.

WHOLE EGG MAYONNAISE

To make mayonnaise, you really only need three ingredients: egg, oil and salt. However, I love the depth and complexity you can achieve by adding anchovy, mustard and garlic. Before you start, make sure all your ingredients are at room temperature as this helps the oil and egg mix together.

INGREDIENTS

3 cloves garlic, peeled and crushed
½ teaspoon sea salt
3 anchovy fillets
1 free-range egg yolk
1 whole egg

1 teaspoon Dijon mustard
125 ml (4 fl oz) olive oil
200 ml (7 fl oz) rice bran oil
1–2 tablespoons lemon juice
sea salt and freshly ground pepper

METHOD

1. Place garlic, salt and anchovies in a food processor and puree to a paste. Add egg yolk, whole egg and Dijon mustard. Process again.
2. With the motor running, gradually add the oil, drop by drop at first, then in a thin, steady stream until thick and emulsified.
3. Once the oil is combined, add the lemon juice to taste and season with salt and pepper, if desired.
4. Transfer any mayonnaise not being used immediately to a clean, sealed jar. Homemade mayonnaise will keep for about 1 week in the refrigerator.

LABNEH

Labneh is a thick, strained Middle Eastern yogurt cheese that is amazingly versatile. I use it tossed through salads, as a toast spread, dipped in warm pita bread or as part of a cheese platter. It's easy and inexpensive (unlike its store-bought versions). Here is a basic recipe with two variations; a chili and garlic topping and a sweet, honey and thyme infused labneh, perfect for a dessert cheese plate or to serve with poached fruit.

INGREDIENTS

1 kg (2 lb) full-cream gluten free yogurt
generous pinch of salt

Chili and garlic
1 garlic clove, minced or finely grated
60 ml (2 fl oz) extra virgin olive oil, or as desired
1 teaspoon chili flakes

Honey and thyme
1–2 tablespoons honey, depending on taste
1 cinnamon quill
2 cloves
2 sprigs thyme

METHOD

1. Set a strainer over a deep bowl, making sure the bottom of the strainer is 5 cm (2 inch) to 10 cm (4 inch) above the bottom of the bowl.
2. Line the strainer with two layers of cheesecloth or muslin cloth.
3. In a large bowl, combine the yogurt and salt, stirring to combine. Pour the yogurt into the lined strainer.
4. Fold the ends of the cheesecloth or cloth over the yogurt and refrigerate for 12–24 hours.
5. Remove the strained cheese (labneh) from the cloth, discarding the liquid (whey) left in the bottom of the bowl.
6. For chili and garlic labneh, place labneh in a serving bowl. Stir through garlic, drizzle with extra virgin olive oil and sprinkle with chili flakes.
7. For honey and thyme labneh, place honey, cinnamon quill, cloves, thyme and 2–3 tablespoons water in a saucepan over low heat. Stir until the honey liquidizes then remove from heat. Set aside and allow to cool completely. Place labneh in a serving bowl and drizzle with cooled honey, thyme and spices over the top.

You can strain the yogurt for a minimum of 4 hours, which will give you with a creamy spread consistency, or up to 72 hours, in which the labneh will be very thick, dense and quite tart. The amount this recipe makes depends on how long you drain the yogurt and what brand of yogurt you use.

HOMEMADE RICOTTA

I love it when you discover a simple kitchen trick—those effortless processes that transform humble foods into something really special. Heating full cream milk and adding some acid (whether it's lemon juice or vinegar) to create gorgeously creamy clumps of ricotta, all in less than 30 minutes, is one of those techniques. Ricotta is such a versatile ingredient—I love it sweet with crumbled walnuts and a drizzle of honey or savoury, with grated garlic and a generous glug of extra virgin olive oil.

INGREDIENTS
75 ml (2½ fl oz) white vinegar
180 ml (6 fl oz) water
1 L (2 pints) full-cream milk
1 teaspoon salt

METHOD
1. In a small pouring jug, combine the vinegar and water. Set aside.
2. Place the milk and salt in a medium saucepan. Stirring constantly, bring to the point of boiling, but do not boil. Remove saucepan from heat. In a slow, steady, circular stream (beginning in the middle and then working out towards the edges), pour the combined vinegar and water into the milk.
3. Let the milk sit, undisturbed, for a few minutes or until the milk has separated to form clumps of milky white curds (ricotta).
4. Set a strainer over a bowl and line the strainer with cheese cloth or muslin.
5. Use a slotted spoon to lift the ricotta and transfer to the colander. Discard whey left in the saucepan (or use in a bath—apparently it is great for your skin).
6. Leave the ricotta to drain for 10–60 minutes. Ricotta will keep in the refrigerator for 2–4 days.

STEAMED COCONUT AND KAFFIR LIME RICE

This is my jazzed-up version of steamed rice. The kaffir lime leaves infuse the rice, giving it a fresh, fragrant lift while the coconut makes it creamy. This dish is a weekly staple in our household as it goes with almost everything and is even delicious on its own. You can freeze kaffir lime leaves – to use the next time you make this dish.

INGREDIENTS

400 g (14 oz) jasmine rice
400 ml (13 fl oz) coconut milk
250 ml (8 fl oz) water
4 kaffir lime leaves
½ teaspoon salt

METHOD

1. To prepare the rice, rinse under cold water a few times until the water runs clear. Drain rice in a colander.
2. Place rice, coconut milk and water in a large saucepan over high heat. Bring to the boil, stirring occasionally. Add kaffir lime leaves and salt and stir to combine. Reduce heat to low. Cover and simmer for 15 minutes. (If using a rice cooker, simply place all ingredients in rice cooker and turn on.)
3. Remove from the heat and let the rice sit covered for 5 minutes. Gently fluff the rice with a fork and serve.

STEAMED JASMINE RICE

Jasmine rice is an aromatic, long grain variety, commonly used in Southeast Asian cooking. I tend to use basmati rice for any Indian recipes and Jasmine rice for any Asian dishes. Jasmine rice has a lovely soft, sticky texture when cooked.

INGREDIENTS
200 g (7 oz) jasmine rice
½ teaspoon sea salt
250 ml (8 fl oz) cold water

METHOD
1. Add the rice and salt to a medium saucepan with cold water.
2. Bring to the boil then reduce heat. Cover and cook for 10–12 minutes or until all the water has been absorbed and the rice is cooked. Remove from heat. Fluff the rice with a fork and set aside for 5 minutes before serving.

INDIAN SPICED PILAU

This pilau (or pilaf) is given an alluring complexity with the addition of yellow mustard seeds, bay leaf, cinnamon and cloves. It works beautifully with any Indian curry, with a side of yogurt raita and, of course, dollops of sweet mango chutney. Yellow mustard seeds can be found at most supermarkets and gourmet delicatessens.

INGREDIENTS

2 tablespoons coconut oil (or olive oil)
1 brown onion, peeled and finely diced
½ teaspoon cumin seeds
½ teaspoon yellow mustard seeds
½ teaspoon salt
¼ teaspoon freshly ground pepper
½ teaspoon ground cumin
½ teaspoon ground coriander

½ teaspoon turmeric powder
300 g (10 oz) basmati rice
1 bay leaf
1 cinnamon sticks
2 cardamom pods, lightly crushed
2 cloves
600 ml (1¼ pints) water

METHOD

1. Place the oil in a frying pan over medium-high heat and sauté onion until soft and lightly golden. Add the cumin seeds and mustard seeds and cook for 1 minute or until fragrant. Add the salt, pepper, cumin, coriander and turmeric and stir to combine. Add the rice and toss well to coat with the spices. Finally, add bay leaf, cinnamon stick, cardamom pods and cloves.
2. Add 600 ml (1¼ pints) water and bring to the boil, stirring regularly. Reduce heat and cover tightly. Wrap the lid with foil to secure tightly.
3. Cook for 15 minutes without lifting the lid. Fluff the grains with a fork, cover and set aside for 5 minutes before serving.

STEAMED SUSHI RICE

The best rice I've ever eaten was in Japan—I could have eaten bowlfuls without anything else. Cooking sushi rice, or Japanese rice, isn't as easy as you'd think. The perfect sushi rice is glossy and tender, but not sticky or gluggy—with a sweet, yet slight vinegar scent. This is a simplified stove-top recipe however, if you've got a rice cooker, it will do a great job too. It's important to use the best quality rice you can afford and, as with risotto rice, check the best before date—fresh rice is best.

INGREDIENTS
460 g (15½ oz) sushi rice
3 tablespoons rice wine vinegar
1 teaspoon superfine (caster) sugar

METHOD
1. Rinse rice under cold running water until water runs clear. Transfer to a saucepan with 1 litre (2 pints) water and bring to the simmer over medium heat. Reduce heat to low. Cover and steam until cooked, about 15 minutes.
2. Combine vinegar and sugar in a small saucepan and heat to low. Cook, stirring constantly, until the sugar has dissolved.
3. Remove saucepan of rice from the heat and drizzle vinegar and sugar over rice. Cover and set aside to allow to cool.

MEASUREMENTS

Mass conversions (rounded out)

Metric	Imperial	Cups
10 g	⅓ oz	
15 g	½ oz	
20 g	¾ oz	
30 g	1 oz	
40 g	1½ oz	
60 g	2 oz	¼ cup
75 g	2½ oz	
90 g	3 oz	
100 g	3½ oz	
125 g	4 oz	½ cup 4 tablespoons
150 g	5 oz	
180 g	6 oz	
200 g	7 oz	
220 g	7¾ oz	
250 g	8 oz	1 cup
280 g	9 oz	
300 g	10 oz	
330 g	11 oz	
350 g	11½ oz	
375 g	12 oz	
400 g	14 oz	
425 g	15 oz	
460 g	15½ oz	
500 g	16 oz (1 lb)	
600 g	1 lb 5 oz	
700 g	1 lb 7 oz	
750 g	1 lb 8 oz	
800 g	1 lb 10 oz	
1 kg	2 lb	
1.5 kg	3 lb	
2 kg	4 lb	

Volume conversions (rounded out)

Metric	Imperial	Cups
30 ml	1 fl oz	
60 ml	2 fl oz	¼ cup
75 ml	2½ fl oz	
90 ml	3 fl oz	⅓ cup
125 ml	4 fl oz	½ cup
150 ml	5 fl oz	⅔ cup
180 ml	6 fl oz	¾ cup
200 ml	6¾ fl oz	
220 ml	7 fl oz	
250 ml	8 fl oz	1 cup
300 ml	10 fl oz	
375 ml	12 fl oz	
400 ml	13 fl oz	
440 ml	14 fl oz	
500 ml	16 fl oz (1 pint)	
625 ml	20 fl oz (1¼ pints)	
750 ml	24 fl oz (1½ pints)	
875 ml	28 fl oz (1¾ pints)	
1 L	32 fl oz (2 pints)	

TEMPERATURES

Celsius	Fahrenheit
100°C	225°F
125°C	250°F
150°C	300°F
160°C	325°F
170°C	325°F
180°C	350°F
190°C	375°F
200°C	400°F
210°C	425°F
220°C	425°F
230°C	450°F
250°C	500°F

ABBREVIATIONS

g	gram
kg	kilogram
mm	millimetre
cm	centimetre
ml	millilitre
°C	degrees Celsius

CAKE TIN SIZES

Metric	Imperial/US
15 cm	6 inches
18 cm	7 inches
20 cm	8 inches
23 cm	9 inches
25 cm	10 inches
28 cm	11 inches

INGREDIENT GLOSSARY

and where to find them

Black rice	Also known as forbidden rice, is an heirloom rice variety that is high in vitamins B, E and minerals potassium and iron. Available from health food stores and most supermarkets.
Chipotle chili in adobo	A rich, smoky and spicy Mexican sauce of smoke-dried japapeno chilies (chipotle). Available from gourmet grocers however you can substitute with Tabasco, Sriracha or any chili sauce.
Dried shrimp (prawns)	a key ingredient in XO sauce, shrimp is dried or dehydrated to create a concentrated shrimp flavor. Available from Asian food stores.
Fish sauce	a sauce made from salted, fermented fish, used in Thai and Vietnamese cuisine. There are various grades available—select a brand that has only two ingredients: fish and salt. Available from supermarkets and Asian grocers.
Freekeh	a young green wheat which is then roasted and cracked. It's a healthy wholegrain, similar to barley in texture and taste but with a slight smokiness.
Gochujang	a Korean chili paste available at some supermarkets and Asian grocers. It can be substituted with any chili sauce.
Harissa	a North African condiment, made from chili, garlic and spices. Harissa is available from most supermarkets, gourmet grocers and delicatessens.
Kecap manis	an Indonesian sweet soy sauce that has a thick, molasses-like consistency. Available from supermarkets and Asian grocers.
Labneh	a thick, strained Middle Eastern yogurt cheese. It is available from select grocers and gourmet delicatessens or see labneh recipe (pg 182).
Mirin	a sweet Japanese cooking wine made from glutinous rice and alcohol. Available in the Asian food aisle at supermarkets or from Asian grocers.
Miso paste	a traditional Japanese paste made from fermenting rice, barley or soy beans. There are many types of miso. White (shiro) miso has a lighter, sweeter taste while soybean and red miso have stronger flavors. Available from supermarkets and Asian grocers.

Nori	an edible seaweed that has been toasted and is sold in sheets, most commonly used for sushi rolls. Available from supermarkets and Asian grocers.
Passata	a fresh tomato puree made by straining ripe tomatoes. The skin and seeds are removed and a thick, pulpy tomato puree remains. Also known as sugo, which is made from crushed tomatoes, so it has more texture. Passata is available from supermarkets.
Pearl barley	is barley that has been processed to remove its hull and bran. Available from health food stores, supermarkets and gourmet grocers.
Pedro Ximénez	a dark, sweet Spanish sherry that is similar in taste to sweet sherry (which makes a good substitute). Available from select liquor stores.
Pomegranate molasses	is pomegranate juice that has been reduced down to create a thick, intensely flavored syrup. Used in a lot of Middle Eastern cooking, it is quite tangy and tart (and not sweet like many other syrups). Available from select supermarkets and gourmet delicatessens.
Quinoa	a South American seed which is cooked like a grain and can be used as you would rice or couscous. Available as tricolor, white, red, brown and black varieties, it can be found at all supermarkets and gourmet delicatessens.
Shaoxing rice wine	is made from fermented rice and is an essential ingredient in Chinese cuisine. It tastes much like dry sherry, which can be used as a substitute. Available from Asian grocers or the Asian aisle of your supermarket.
Shichimi togarashi	is a Japanese spice blend that can be found in selected supermarkets and Asian food stores. If unavailable, substitute with a sprinkle of chili powder.
Shiso	also known as perilla, shiso is a member of the mint family and is available from select greengrocers.
Shrimp paste	a pungent paste made by grinding salted and fermented shrimp and a key ingredient in Southeast Asian cooking. It is available from most supermarkets and Asian grocers.
Soba noodles	are Japanese noodles made from buckwheat. Some varieties are also made with wheat flour so if you're gluten intolerant, check the ingredient list. Available from supermarkets and Asian grocers.
Speck	originating in Italy, speck is a firm slab of smoked and cured ham that is available from select supermarkets and delicatessens. Substitute with pancetta or streaky bacon.

Squid ink the ink found in the sac of a squid. The ink is extracted during the preparation of the squid and has a delicate flavor. It is available fresh from your local fishmonger or in sachets or jars from gourmet delicatessens.

Sriracha a hot Thai sauce made from a paste of chili peppers, distilled vinegar, garlic, sugar and salt. Available from most supermarkets and Asian grocers.

Sumac a ground spice made from dried red berries, it is used in Middle Eastern cooking. Sumac can be bought at any gourmet grocer or delicatessen.

Swiss chard also known as chard or silverbeet, this deep green spinach has tall, broad leaves and a thick, crunchy stalk. Available from most supermarkets and gourmet grocers.

Tahini a paste made from ground sesame seeds and used in a lot of Middle Eastern dishes. There are two varieties available; hulled tahini has the outer husk removed while unhulled includes the husk and while it is the least refined, it can be slightly bitter. Available from health food stores, supermarkets and gourmet grocers. Tahini tends to separate as it sits especially if left in the refrigerator—the easiest way to combine the two is to sit the jar upside down for 15 minutes before you use the tahini.

Wonton wrappers thin sheets of dough, available fresh or frozen, commonly used to make dumplings. Available from most supermarkets and Asian grocers.

INDEX

ACKNOWLEDGEMENTS

With eternal gratitude

First, to my husband and best friend, Andrew, thank you for your constant support, eternal patience and unique sense of humour. You've not only edited this entire book but, quite possibly, everything I've ever written. Thank you for making me laugh every day.

To my parents; Dad, thank you for patiently trying kale salads and bowls of chia pudding, even though you'd much prefer a lamb chop. You have given me every opportunity in life and supported me through every struggle and success. Mum, where do I start? Thank you for countless trips to the supermarket to buy forgotten ingredients, testing endless recipes and making notes but most of all, thank you for giving me my love of cooking.

To Hugh, I will love you forever and I miss you every single day. I know you have been with me every step of way and you would be more excited about this book than anyone else.

To Sam, Kate, Harriett, Thomas and William, I love you all to the moon and back. To my grandparents, Nanny and Hans, Granny and Grandfather, I'm so lucky to have you all in my life.

My beautiful friends, many of whom I have known since I was a little tot, your friendships mean the world to me.

To the talented duo, stylist Jane Graystone and photographer Kyle Manning, who have worked tirelessly to make the book look so beautiful, you have my eternal gratitude. I would like to acknowledge various prop suppliers; Fairweather Design, Café Graze in Walcha and Weswal Gallery in Tamworth. A huge thank you to Coles Supermarkets for supplying all the ingredients for the photo shoot.

To Luke Mangan, for taking the time out of your busy schedule to write the foreword to this book – I can't thank you enough for your encouragement and support. Your success and your humility are an inspiration to everyone who is passionate about food.

A huge thank you to the team at New Holland, particularly Diane Ward, who has patiently answered endless questions and guided me seamlessly through this whole process.

ABOUT THE AUTHOR

Anna Lisle is a lifestyle journalist and a passionate cook. She has combined these two passions to write Bowl&Fork, a book that brings together her extensive knowledge and her love of seasonal, wholesome and delicious food.

As a food journalist, Anna has worked for various newspapers, magazines, radio programs and television shows. Anna is Senior Editor for Best Restaurants. As part of her role, she regularly attends restaurant openings, food and wine fairs and hospitality media events.

Along with her mother, Cathy, Anna runs a cooking school with intimate, hands-on classes that focuses on a paddock-to-plate philosophy in rural Australia. Anna and Cathy also produce a gourmet granola and muesli range.

First published in 2015 by New Holland Publishers Pty Ltd
London • Sydney • Auckland

The Chandlery Unit 704 50 Westminster Bridge Road London SE1 7QY United Kingdom
1/66 Gibbes Street Chatswood NSW 2067 Australia
5/39 Woodside Ave Northcote, Auckland 0627 New Zealand

www.newhollandpublishers.com

ISBN 9781742577838

Managing Director: Fiona Schultz
Publisher: Diane Ward
Project Editor: Susie Stevens
Designer: Andrew Quinlan
Photographer: Kyle Manning
Stylist: Jane Graystone
Production Director: Olga Dementiev
Printer: Toppan Leefung Printing Limited

10 9 8 7 6 5 4 3 2 1

Keep up with New Holland Publishers on Facebook
www.facebook.com/NewHollandPublishers